NuWave Oven Cookbook

Over 100 Quick and Easy Recipes

Fry, Bake, Grill or Roast

By April Stewart

Copyright © 2017 April Stewart

Disclaimer

This book is designed to provide condensed information. It is not intended to reprint all the information that is otherwise available, but instead to complement, amplify and supplement other texts. You are urged to read all the available material, learn as much as possible and tailor the information to your individual needs.

Every effort has been made to make this book as complete and as accurate as possible. However, there may be mistakes, both typographical and in content. Therefore, this text should be used only as a general guide and not as the ultimate source of information. The purpose of this book is to educate.

The author or the publisher shall have neither liability nor responsibility to any person or entity regarding any loss or damage caused, or alleged to have been caused, directly or indirectly, by the information contained in this book.

Table of Contents

Introduction

Breakfast Recipes

Appetizer Recipes

Beef Recipes

Poultry Recipes

Dessert Recipes

Conclusion

Introduction

Life has taken a healthier turn. Today we no longer want to eat deep fried pieces of vegetables or meats. Rather, we want to switch them out for healthy, but equally delicious meals. Most of these healthy and delicious meals require you to slave over them for hours in the kitchen.

But, what if I tell you that you can prepare healthy and extremely delicious food in the confines of your kitchen without slaving in the kitchen for hours?

Presenting to you: the NuWave Oven.

The NuWave oven is a new revolutionary technology that combines three different cooking methods to give you a kitchen appliance that cooks food faster and in a healthier manner. The NuWave oven uses its patented technology that combines the power of infrared, conduction and convection to provide you with quicker and healthier meals. The NuWave oven is a highly efficient device that not only cooks food 50% faster as compared to a normal oven, but also uses about 85% less energy when compared to a regular oven.

The NuWave oven is an all in one device in which you can grill, roast, bake, steam, broil or barbeque your foods. You do not need to preheat it or defrost frozen foods before cooking while using the NuWave oven. Pop them in and you are good to go!

Food cooked in the NuWave oven is juicy and succulent, and

best of all the fat drains away! Yes, you read that right! Due to its innovative 3-heat technology, the food cooks in a closed environment. This ensures that the juices (and nutrients) are retained within the food, while the excess fat drips away.

It is fast and energy efficient and it also makes your food healthier. But, can it cook all kinds of foods and not just a specific type of food?

Yes! You can cook all kinds of proteins, vegetables, lentils, grains, and dairy products in the NuWave oven. From breakfast to appetizers to mains to desserts – the NuWave oven can cook them all! Unlike most infrared technology where your meat cooks, but remains un-browned, the NuWave's patented 3 heat technology ensures that your food browns and becomes crispy, not just making it healthy, but making it appetizing too!

This book contains over 100 different types of recipes that will help you with your NuWave oven. All the recipes are easy to make and do not require a lot of prep work. All the ingredients used in the recipes in this book are easily available in most kitchens or pantries and will not require you to head to specialty stores!

I would like to take this opportunity to thank you for purchasing this book and I hope you find the recipes as delicious and healthy as I do.

Breakfast Recipes

1. Delicious Sausage And Egg Breakfast "Pudding"

Servings: Serves 2 - 3

Ingredients:

- 1 tablespoon olive oil
- 2 mushrooms, sliced
- 1/4 cup leek, sliced
- 1 green onion, sliced
- 2 eggs
- 1 cup turkey breakfast sausage, large diced
- 1/2 cup heavy cream
- 1/2 cup Gouda cheese, shredded
- 3/8 cup milk
- 2 cups Hawaiian bread, diced into 1-inch cubes
- Freshly ground black pepper, to taste
- Kosher salt, to taste

Directions:

1. Combine the olive oil, mushrooms, turkey sausage, leeks and onions together in a large 10 inch baking pan.

2. Sprinkle generous amounts of salt and pepper to season.

3. Place the prepared baking pan on the 3-inch cooking rack and cook for about 10 to 12 minutes at 300 degrees Fahrenheit. Stop the oven around the 5 to 6 minute mark and stir well to ensure even cooking.

4. While the sausage mixture is baking, place the eggs, milk, heavy cream and Gouda cheese together in a large mixing bowl. Whisk well until all the ingredients are well incorporated. Keep aside.

5. Once the sausage mix is done cooking, leave the baking pan in the oven to rest.

6. Place the bread cubes in the egg mixture and mix well until the bread is incorporated.

7. Remove the sausage mix from the oven and pour the prepared egg and bread mixture over the cooked sausage. Mix well until well combined.

8. Place the prepared baking pan on the 1-inch cooking rack and back for 50 to 55 minutes at 300 degrees Fahrenheit.

9. Bake until it gets a brown crust.

10. Once done, let the dish rest in the oven for a few minutes.

11. Serve hot topped with some fresh herbs or salsa of your choice.

12. Enjoy!

2. Delicious Spicy Pork And Egg Breakfast Skillet

Servings: Serves 12

Ingredients:

- 1 1/2 pounds new potatoes, washed
- 1 1/2 cups green or red peppers, small diced
- 1/2 cup leeks, sliced
- 2 teaspoons garlic, minced
- 2 tablespoons dark chili powder
- 4 tablespoons olive oil
- 2 cups spicy pork sausage, diced
- 4 eggs
- 1 cup pepper jack cheese
- Freshly ground black pepper, to taste
- Kosher salt, to taste

Directions:

1. Combine the potatoes, peppers, olive oil, salt, leeks, garlic, chili powder and pepper together in a large mixing bowl. Mix lightly until all the ingredients are well combined.
2. Pour the prepared mix into a large 10-inch baking pan.
3. Place the baking pan on a 3-inch cooking rack and cook for about 10 to 12 minutes at 350 degrees Fahrenheit.
4. Add the spicy pork sausage pieces into the baking pan and mix well.

5. Return the baking pan into the oven on the 3-inch cooking rack and bake for about 6 to 8 minutes a 350 degrees Fahrenheit.
6. Add in a layer of pepper jack cheese and continue baking on 350 degrees Fahrenheit for another 3 to 4 minutes or until the cheese has completely melted.
7. Crack the eggs over the melted cheese and return the baking pan to the oven.
8. Reduce the cooking temperature to 320 degrees Fahrenheit and cook for another 5 to 7 minutes or until the eggs are done.
9. Serve hot.
10. Enjoy!

3. Delicious Pecan And Maple Syrup Cinnamon Rolls

Servings: Serves 1

Ingredients:

- 1 ounce (1/4 stick) unsalted butter
- 1/4 cup maple syrup
- 1/4 cup light or medium brown sugar
- 1/4 teaspoon cinnamon
- 1/2 (8-ounce) bag chopped pecans
- 1/4 teaspoon vanilla
- 1 package raw cinnamon breakfast rolls

Directions:

1. Place the butter, maple syrup, vanilla, brown sugar, cinnamon and pecans together in a large 10 inch baking pan. Mix well until all the ingredients are well incorporated.
2. Place the prepared baking pan on the 3-inch cooking rack and bake for 6 to 12 minutes on 350 degrees Fahrenheit.
3. Once done, add the raw cinnamon breakfast roll dough to the pan with the cinnamon side up.
4. Cover the pan with an aluminum foil and fold it over the edges firmly in order to seal it.
5. Return the pan to the oven and continue cooking for another 10 to 12 minutes at 350 degrees Fahrenheit.
6. Carefully remove the foil from the pan and continue cooking for another 10 to 12 minutes.
7. Place a serving plate upside down on the baking pan and flip it over to unmold.
8. Let the rolls cool for about 5 to 7 minutes before serving.

4. Quick And Easy Steak And Eggs With Cheese Stuffed Tomatoes

Servings: Serves 2

Ingredients:

- 2 (4-ounce) sirloin steaks
- 4 tablespoons parmesan cheese, grated
- 1 tomato, halved, seeds removed
- 2 tablespoons butter
- Seasoned salt, to taste
- 4 large eggs
- 2 scallions, thinly sliced

Directions:

1. Slice about 1/4 of the tomato from the top of each tomato half. Lightly silver the bottom of the tomato so that it can stand upright without tumbling over.
2. Place the tomato halves and the sirloin steaks on a 3-inch cooking rack.
3. Add the grated Parmesan cheese to the tomatoes.
4. Cook the steak and tomatoes on 420 degrees Fahrenheit.
5. The steak should be cooked for about 4 to 5 minutes on each side if you want a medium done steak.
6. The tomato halves need to be cooked for about 8 minutes.
7. Place a large 10.5-inch skillet on a medium flame. Add in the butter and heat for about a minute or until the butter has completely melted.
8. Add the eggs to the hot butter and cook until the whites are completely set and the yolks become firm. This should take about 3 to 4 minutes.

9. Once the steaks are done, season generously with seasoned salt.
10. Place the steaks on 2 serving plates.
11. Place the cheese stuffed tomato halves on each plates.
12. Top each steak with 2 fried eggs each.
13. Serve hot, topped with some sliced scallions.
14. Enjoy!

5. Lip Smacking Spinach Havarti Frittata with Oven Dried Herbed Plum Tomatoes

Servings: Serves 4
Ingredients:

Frittata Ingredients:

- 4 whole eggs
- 4 cups grated Havarti
- 1 cup whole milk
- 4 tablespoons extra virgin olive oil
- 2 cloves garlic, minced
- 4 cups fresh baby spinach
- Pepper, to taste
- Salt, to taste

Oven-Dried Tomatoes Ingredients:

- 12 plum tomatoes, cut in half
- 1/8 cup Kosher salt
- 1/8 cup sugar
- 1 tablespoon Herb de Provence

Directions:

Frittata Directions:

1. Heat a large 10.5-inch frying pan over a medium high flame. Add in the olive oil and heat.
2. Add in the baby spinach and generously sprinkle salt and pepper to taste.
3. Cook for about 3 to 4 minutes or until the spinach wilts around the edges.
4. Transfer the spinach into a bowl and refrigerate immediately for rapid cooling.

5. In another mixing bowl, combine together eggs, cheese, garlic, milk and spinach together. Whisk well until well combined.
6. Add in salt and pepper to taste.
7. Pour the prepared frittata mixture into the liner pan and bake for about 35 to 40 minutes at 375 degrees Fahrenheit.
8. Once done, prick the center of the frittata with a toothpick. If the toothpick comes out clean the frittata is done, if not, continue cooking.

Oven Dried Tomatoes Directions:

1. Remove the seeds from all the plum tomato halves.
2. In a small mixing bowl, combine together the sugar, Herb de Provence and salt together. Mix lightly until well combined.
3. Sprinkle the prepared mix over the plum tomato halves, ensuring that each tomato gets a generous helping of the seasoning mix.
4. Arrange the seasoned plum tomato halves in a single layer in dehydration trays with their pulp side up.
5. Set the temperature of the dehydrator to 120 degrees and cook for a good 7 to 8 hours.

To Serve:

1. Divide the frittata into 4 equal parts.
2. Place each quarter on a serving plate.
3. Serve hot, topped with the dehydrated herbed tomatoes.
4. Enjoy!

6. Melt In Your Mouth Cranberry Scones

Servings: Serves 12

Ingredients:

- 4 cups all-purpose flour
- 2 tablespoons baking powder
- 1/2 cup packed brown sugar
- 1/2 teaspoon ground nutmeg
- 1/2 cup butter, chilled and diced
- 1/2 teaspoon salt
- 2 cups fresh cranberries, roughly chopped
- 2 grated zest of two oranges
- 2/3 cup white sugar
- 1 cup chopped walnuts
- 2 eggs
- 1 1/2 cups half and half cream

Directions:

1. Place the flour, baking powder, salt, brown sugar and nutmeg together in a large mixing bowl. Whisk using a wire whisk so that all the ingredients are well combined.
2. Add the butter to the bowl and mix well until the mixture resembles coarse sand. Keep aside.
3. In another bowl, mix the cranberries with the sugar and toss well until well coated.
4. Add the sugarcoated cranberries, walnuts and orange zest to the coarse flour -mix. Lightly mix until just combined. Keep aside.
5. In another mixing bowl place the cream and eggs together. Whisk well until the eggs are well incorporated.

6. Slowly pour the egg and cream mixture into the flour mix, mixing well after each addition.
7. Keep mixing until you form a soft dough.
8. Knead the dough with your hands about 5 to 6 times. Make sure you do not over knead it.
9. Divide the dough into four quarters
10. Place one quarter of the dough on a lightly floured workstation.
11. Roll the dough into a large circle, about 6 inches in diameter.
12. Cut the circle into 6 wedges.
13. Repeat with the remaining quarters until you have 24 wedges.
14. Rub some oil on the liner pan or spray it lightly with some cooking spray.
15. Place the Extender Ring on the base of your NuWave Oven Elite.
16. Place about 6 wedges around the perimeter of the prepared liner pan.
17. Bake for about 20 to 22 minutes at 300 degrees Fahrenheit.
18. Once the timer is up, remove the scones immediately from the oven and allow the scones to cool slightly before transferring to a cooling rack.
19. Repeat with the remaining wedges.
20. Serve warm.
21. Enjoy!

7. Pasta and Cheese Frittata

Serving: Serves 2 - 3

Ingredients:

- 1/6 cup ricotta
- 2 large eggs
- 1/2 cup grated parmesan cheese
- 8 slices bacon
- 1/2 tablespoon olive oil
- 1/4 cup tomato sauce
- 1 1/2 cups of pasta (any kind) spaghetti, linguine, macaroni, Orecchiette (cooked)

Directions:

1. Place the bacon slices on a 4-inch cooking rack in a single layer. Cook on the HI setting for about 8 minutes.
2. Remove the bacon slices from the oven and cool before crumbling. You should have about ½ cup worth of crumbles.
3. Combine together the ricotta, eggs, Parmesan, bacon crumbles, olive oil, tomato sauce and pasta together in a large mixing bowl. Mix well until the pasta is well coated.
4. Lightly grease a large inch baking dish with some butter or spray with some cooking oil.
5. Pour the prepared pasta mix into the greased baking pan and use the back of a spoon or a spatula to press the mixture into the bottom of the pan.
6. Place the prepared baking pan on the 4-inch cooking rack and bake for about 12 to 15 minutes or until the top gets a dark brown, crust like texture.

7. During the last 7 minutes of cooking, cover the baking pan with a foil to prevent over browning.
8. Place a serving plate over the baking pan upside down and flip the baking pan over. Lightly tap to de-mold.
9. Serve hot.
10. Enjoy!

8. Nest Egg with Manchego

Servings: Serves 2

Ingredients:

- 2 slices of bread
- 2 eggs
- 2 teaspoons butter or cooking spray
- 6 tablespoons Manchego cheese

Directions:

1. Use a small round cookie cutter to remove a circle of bread from the slice.
2. Use your fingers to flatten the bread slice.
3. Apply a thin layer of butter on both sides of the bread.
4. Place the bread slices in the bottom of an oven safe baking dish.
5. Place the baking dish on a 3-inch cooking rack.
6. Carefully crack an egg into the hole in the bread slice; making sure that the egg doesn't spill out.
7. Sprinkle some black pepper on the egg and cover with a layer of Manchego cheese.
8. Repeat with the remaining bread slice.
9. Bake at 375 degrees Fahrenheit for about 7 to 10 minutes or until the egg is done to your preference.
10. Serve hot with a side of fresh fruit and some crispy bacon.
11. Enjoy!

9. Brown Sugar And Corn Syrup French Toast

Serving: Serves 1 - 2

Ingredients:

- 1/8 cup butter
- 1/2 tablespoon corn syrup
- 1/4 cup packed brown sugar
- 3 to 4 slices of (1-inch thick) bread, whole wheat or white
- 3/8 cup milk or half and half
- 2 large eggs
- 1/8 teaspoon salt
- 1/2 teaspoon vanilla

Directions:

1. Heat a small sized saucepan over a medium flame.
2. Add in the butter and heat until melted.
3. Once the butter has liquefied, add in the corn syrup and brown sugar.
4. Continue heating until it gets a smooth consistency.
5. Pour the prepared mix into the bottom of an 8-inch by 8-inch baking pan or a round 10-inch baking pan.
6. Remove the crusts of the bread slices and place them in the bottom of the pan in a single layer. You may have to lightly flatten the bread slices so that they all fit easily in the pan.
7. Combine together the eggs, vanilla, salt, half and half or milk in a medium sized mixing bowl. Whisk well until all the ingredients are well incorporated.
8. Pour the prepared egg mixture over the bread slices.
9. Cover the pan and refrigerate for at least an hour, but it is preferred to let it rest overnight.

10. Place the prepared baking dish on the 1-inch cooking rack and bake on the HI power level for about 30 minutes.
11. If you feel that the top is browning too fast, cover the pan with some aluminum foil.
12. Serve warm with a side of fresh fruits.
13. Enjoy!

10. Instant Smoked Salmon Quesadilla With Cream Cheese And Chives

Serving: Serves 2

Ingredients:

- 4 (8-inch) flour tortillas
- Freshly ground black pepper, to taste
- 1/4 pound good-quality smoked salmon
- 3 ounces whipped cream cheese and chives (approximately 6 tablespoons)
- 2 teaspoons olive oil

Directions:

1. Pace 2 flour tortillas on a flat working surface.
2. Spread each tortilla with about 3 tablespoons of the whipped cream cheese and chives. Make sure you leave about ½ inch from all the edges.
3. Slice the smoked salmon into 1-inch strips and divide into two equal halves.
4. Spread each half of the salmons onto the cream cheese covered tortillas.
5. Sprinkle some freshly ground black pepper over the salmon pieces.
6. Place the remaining tortillas over the salmon and lightly press down.
7. Spread about ½ teaspoon of the olive oil on each tortilla and flip onto the 4-inch cooking rack.
8. Brush the remaining oil over the tortillas.
9. Cook on the HI power level for about 4 to 6 minutes on each side.
10. Slice into manageable pieces and serve hot with a side of your favorite salsa.
11. Enjoy!

Appetizer Recipes

11. Oven Fried Ravioli

Serving: Serves 2

Ingredients:

- 1/4 cup all-purpose flour
- Pepper, to taste
- Salt, to taste
- 2 eggs
- Basil (optional)
- 1/4 cup breadcrumbs
- 5 ravioli, frozen
- 1 tablespoon chopped parsley
- 1 tablespoon parmesan cheese
- Marinara sauce (optional)

Directions:

1. Sieve together the salt, flour and pepper together in a small mixing bowl. Keep aside.

2. In another small mixing bowl, crack open the eggs and whisk well until lightly frothy.
3. In a third small mixing bowl, add in the basil and breadcrumbs and mix well until well combined.
4. Place the ravioli in the flour mix and toss well until well coated.
5. Dunk the flour covered ravioli into the whisked egg and shake of the excess.
6. Finally, roll the egg-covered ravioli in the breadcrumb mixture.
7. Repeat with the remaining ravioli.
8. Place the breaded ravioli in a single layer on the 3-inch cooking rack.
9. Cook for about 8 to 10 minutes at 400 degrees Fahrenheit.
10. Once the ravioli is cooked through, top with parsley and Parmesan.
11. Serve hot with some marinara sauce.
12. Enjoy!

12. Cheese Stuffed Mushroom Caps

Servings: Yields 12 mushrooms

Ingredients:

- 1/2 garlic clove, finely chopped
- 2 tablespoons olive oil, divided
- 1/4 cup finely chopped roasted red pepper
- 1/2 teaspoon finely chopped fresh sage
- 2 ounces shredded mozzarella cheese
- Pinch salt
- 12 small mushroom caps, stems removed

Directions:

1. Combine together garlic, 1-tablespoon olive oil, salt, red pepper and sage together in a medium sized mixing bowl. Mix well until well combined.
2. Add in the shredded mozzarella cheese and keep mixing.
3. In another bowl, place the mushroom caps. Pour the remaining olive oil over them and toss well until well coated.
4. Spoon the prepared cheese mixture into the oil coated mushroom caps.
5. Place the stuffed mushroom caps in a single layer on the 3-inch cooking rack.
6. Bake for about 5 to 7 minutes at 350 degrees Fahrenheit.
7. When done, remove the mushrooms from the oven and cool until handle able.
8. Serve warm with a condiment of your choice.
9. Enjoy!

13. Delicious Caramel Glaze Chicken Skewers

Serving: Serves 1

Ingredients:

- 1 tablespoon fish sauce
- 1/2 tablespoon orange juice
- 1/2 tablespoon light brown sugar
- 1 3/4 pounds skinless chicken breasts, cut into 1-inch chunks
- 1/8 cup white sesame seeds
- 6 inch bamboo skewers
- 1/6 cup sliced almonds
- 1/8 cup black sesame seeds

Ingredients for the Caramel Glaze:

- 1/6 cup fish sauce
- 1/3 cup light brown sugar
- 1/6 cup orange juice
- 1/6 cup rice wine vinegar
- 1 tablespoon honey
- 1/2 tablespoon garlic, minced
- 1/2 (1-inch) piece fresh ginger, minced
- 1 shallot, chopped

Directions:

1. In a small mixing bowl, whisk together the fish sauce, orange juice and brown sugar using a wire whisk. Whisk well until all the ingredients are incorporated.
2. Soak the bamboo skewers in some warm water for 6 to 8 hours.
3. Thread the chicken pieces on to the bamboo skewers.

4. Place the skewers in a large bowl and pour the prepared marinade over them. Toss well to coat.
5. Cover the bow and refrigerate for about 3 to 4 hours.
6. In another bowl, combine together the remaining fish sauce, brown sugar, orange juice, rice wine vinegar, honey, garlic, ginger and shallot together. Whisk well until well combined.
7. Combine the almonds and sesame seeds and spread in an even layer in the bottom of a pizza liner pan. If you do not have a pizza liner pan, just use a small cookie sheet.
8. Place the pizza liner pan on the 3-inch cooking rack and toast for about 3 to 5 minutes on 350 degrees Fahrenheit. Keep aside.
9. Place the marinated chicken skewers on the 3-inch cooking rack and lightly brush the prepared caramel glaze over them.
10. Bake for about 7 to 10 minutes at 350 degrees Fahrenheit.
11. Flip the chicken skewers over and brush some caramel glaze over them. Continue baking for another 7 to 10 minutes.
12. Place the prepared chicken skewers on a serving platter and serve hot topped with the prepared toasted almonds and sesame seeds.
13. Enjoy!

14. Cheesy Zucchini, Corn And Black Bean Quesadillas

Serving: Serves 2

Ingredients:

- 1/2 small zucchini, grated and drained
- 1/2 small red onion, chopped
- 1/2 cup frozen corn, defrosted and drained
- 1 jalapeno pepper, seeded and chopped
- 1/4 teaspoon salt
- 1/2 (15-ounce) can black beans, drained and rinsed
- 1/8 teaspoon freshly ground black pepper
- 1/2 pound Monterey Jack cheese, grated
- 1/2 teaspoon chili powder
- 1 tablespoon vegetable oil
- 4 (8-inch) flour tortillas

Directions:

1. Place the zucchini, onion, beans, pepper, corn, jalapenos, salt and chili powder together in a large mixing bowl. Toss well until all the ingredients are well coated with the seasoning.
2. Add in the cheese and mix well.
3. Place the tortillas on a floured flat work surface.
4. Scoop about ¼ of the prepared vegetable filling onto one half of a tortilla. Spread into and even layer using the back of a spoon, ensuring that the filling doesn't touch the edge of the tortilla.
5. Fold the tortillas in half over the filling.
6. Place the prepared quesadillas on the 3-inch cooking rack and cook for about 4 to 5 minutes per side at 350 degrees Fahrenheit.

7. Cut the quesadillas into halves and serve warm with your favorite condiment.
8. Enjoy!

15. Apple Jelly Glazed Spicy Chicken Wings

Serving: Serves 1 - 2

Ingredients:

- 1 tablespoon all-purpose flour
- 1/4 teaspoon dried garlic
- 1/2 teaspoon salt
- 1/4 teaspoon dried onion
- 1 pound chicken wings
- 1/2 teaspoon smoked paprika
- 1 1/4 tablespoons cayenne pepper sauce
- 1 tablespoon apple jelly, melted
- 1 tablespoon unsalted butter, melted
- Chipotle peppers in adobo sauce

Directions:

1. Combine the flour, garlic, paprika, salt and onion together in a large mixing bowl.
2. Add the chicken to the flour mix and toss well until well coated.
3. Place the flour coated chicken thighs on the 3-inch cooking rack.
4. Pop the rack into the oven and bake the chicken for about 40 to 45 minutes at 350 degrees Fahrenheit. Flip the chicken over around the 20-minute mark for even browning.
5. While the chicken roasts in the oven, place the hot sauce, butter, apple jelly and chipotle peppers together in a small mixing bowl. Whisk well until combined.
6. Place the roasted chicken wings on a serving platter and drizzle the prepared sauce over them.
7. Serve hot with a side of pan-fried veggies.
8. Enjoy!

16. NuWave Style Cheesy Nachos

Serving: Serves 2

Ingredients:

- 1/2 bag tortilla chips
- 1/2 pound cooked ground beef
- 1/2 package taco seasoning
- 2 tomatoes, diced
- 1/2 can sliced olives
- 1/2 jar pickled jalapenos
- 1/2 jar salsa
- 1/4 cup sour cream
- 1/2 bag shredded cheddar cheese

Directions:

1. Pour the tortilla chips directly into the liner pan.
2. Combine the ground beef with the taco seasoning and then spread over the taco chips in an even layer.
3. In a small mixing bowl combine together the tomatoes, jalapenos, sour cream, olives and salsa.
4. Mix well and pour over the ground beef.
5. Alternatively, you can layer each individual ingredient beginning with tomato, followed by olives and jalapenos, topped with a layer of salsa topped with a layer of sour cream.
6. Pour the cheese over the nachos and pop the liner pan into your NuWave Oven.
7. Bake at 350 degrees Fahrenheit for about 10 to 15 minutes.
8. Let the nachos cool before serving.
9. Enjoy!

17. Cheesy Garlic Bread

Serving: Serves 2

Ingredients:

- ½ loaf Italian bread sliced in half
- 1 clove garlic, minced
- 3 tablespoons olive oil
- 1/4 teaspoon dried oregano
- 1/2 cup shredded Asiago
- 1 tablespoon grated Parmesan cheese
- 1/2 cup Mozzarella cheese

Directions:

1. Combine the olive oil, oregano and garlic together in a small bow. Whisk well until well combined.
2. Use a pastry brush to brush the cut sides of the bread with prepared herbed olive oil on it.
3. In another mixing bowl combine the Asiago cheese, Parmesan cheese and Mozzarella cheese together.
4. Divide the cheese equally amongst the bread slices, sprinkling generously on the cut sides.
5. Place the cheese covered bread on the 1-inch cooking rack and bake on the HI power setting for about 12 to 14 minutes or until the cheese is melted and bubbly.
6. Slice the garlic bread and serve immediately topped with some red chili flakes.
7. Enjoy!

18. Cheesy Bacon And Tater Tot Bombs

Serving: Serves 2

Ingredients:

- 1 cup frozen tater tots, brought to room temperature
- 2 slices bacon, quartered
- 1/2 ounce sharp cheddar cheese, cut into 1/4-inch squares
- 1/2 tablespoon chopped parsley (optional)
- 1/8 cup brown sugar

Directions:

1. Place a tater tot on a cheese square.
2. Holding them into place, wrap a single bacon slice around both tightly.
3. Place the brown sugar in a flat plate.
4. Roll the bacon covered tater tot and cheese squares in the brown sugar, pressing lightly, until covered in a layer of brown sugar.
5. Carefully arrange the tater tots in the liner pan in a single layer, with their seam side down.
6. Bake for about 25 to 30 minutes at 350 degrees Fahrenheit.
7. Around the 12-minute mark, flip the tater tot over to ensure even browning.
8. Top with some parsley and serve hot.
9. Enjoy!

19. Sweet And Spicy Roasted Nuts

Servings: Yields 2 cups

Ingredients:

- 1 1/2 tablespoons sugar
- 1/2 teaspoon paprika
- 1/4 teaspoon salt
- 1/2 teaspoon ground cinnamon
- Pinch ground cloves
- 1/4 teaspoon ground cumin
- 1/2 large egg white
- 1 cup pecans
- 1 cup walnuts

Directions:

1. Combine together the sugar, paprika, salt, ground cinnamon, ground cloves and ground cumin together in a small mixing bowl. Keep aside.
2. Whisk the egg white until lightly frothy.
3. Add the pecans and walnuts to the whisked egg white and mix well.
4. Pour the prepared spice mix onto the egg white coated nuts and toss well until well coated.
5. Spread the prepared nut mix in the bottom of the liner pan and cook for about 25 minutes at 350 degrees Fahrenheit.
6. Pause the oven around the 12-minute mark and mix well.
7. Rest in the oven until the pan is cool enough to handle.
8. Cool the nuts completely before serving.

9. Store the leftover nuts (if any) in an airtight jar, at room temperature, away from direct sunlight. The shelf life of these nuts is 3 days.
10. Enjoy!

20. Cheesy Toasted Pita Chips With A Garlic And Artichoke Dip

Serving: Serves 6

Ingredients:

- 1/2 (12-ounce) can medium diced artichokes, drained
- 2 cups Monterey Jack cheese, shredded and divided
- 1 tablespoon fresh garlic, minced
- 1/2 cup heavy cream
- 1/8 cup parmesan cheese
- 1/4 cup mayonnaise
- 1/4 cup bread crumbs
- White pepper, to taste
- Salt, to taste
- 1/2 package of fresh pita chips
- 1/8 cup parmesan cheese
- 1/8 cup olive oil
- 1/4 cup finely chopped parsley

Directions:

1. Combine the diced artichokes, 1-cup Monterey Jack cheese, cream, breadcrumbs, pepper, garlic, mayonnaise, Parmesan cheese and salt together in a large mixing bowl. Mix well until all the ingredients are well combined.
2. Pour this mix into a large 10 inch baking pan and even the top out using the back of a spoon or a spatula.
3. Top with the remaining Monterey Jack cheese.
4. Place the baking dish on the 1-inch cooking rack and bake on the HI power setting for about 10 to 12 minutes or until the filling is hot and the top has browned.

5. While the dip cooks, cut the pita bread into about 6 pieces per slice.
6. Place the pita chips in a bowl and pour the olive oil over them. Toss well to coat.
7. Place the chips on the 4-inch cooking rack in a single layer and toast for about 3 to 4 minutes on the HI power setting or until evenly browned.
8. Place the toasted pita chips in a bowl and top with parsley, pepper, Parmesan cheese and salt. Toss well to coat.
9. Serve immediately with the prepared dip on the side.
10. Enjoy!

21. New Orleans Style Crab Cakes

Serving: Serves 1

Ingredients:

- 1 tablespoon Dijon mustard
- 1/2 cup beef broth
- 1/4 cup grain mustard
- 1/8 cup white wine
- 8 ounces pasteurized crab meat (lump or claw meat)
- 1/2 cup heavy cream
- 1/2 tablespoon chives, finely diced
- 1/3 cup celery, finely diced
- 1 tablespoon red pepper, finely diced
- 1 1/2 ounces, Japanese Panko breadcrumbs
- Salt, to taste
- 1/2 egg
- Old Bay Seasoning, to taste
- Pepper, to taste

Directions:

1. Heat a 3.5 to 4 quart pot over a medium flame. Add in the grain mustard, white wine, Dijon mustard and beef broth to it. Continue heating until the liquid is lightly bubbling.
2. Pour in the cream and mix well until well blended.
3. Lower the heat to a medium low and heat for another 10 minutes or until the sauce is thick enough to coat the back of a spoon.
4. Take the sauce off the heat and keep aside, but ensure it remains warm.
5. In a mixing bowl, combine together the crabmeat, red pepper, Panko, salt, Old Bay seasoning, chives, celery,

egg, and pepper together. Fold well until all the ingredients are well combined.

6. Divide the mix into three equal parts and make crab patties that are 1-inch thick and 3-inches wide from each third.
7. Tear sheet of foil large enough to cover your cooking rack. Cover the 1-inch cooking rack with the foil and grease the foil with some butter or spray some cooking spray over it.
8. Place the prepared 3 crab cakes on the greased foil.
9. Bake on the HI power setting for 5 to 7 minutes, flipping it over around the 3-minute mark.
10. Serve hot with some mustard sauce on the side.
11. Enjoy!

22. Cheesy Beer Scones

Servings: Yields 4 scones

Ingredients:

- 1 1/2cups all-purpose flour
- 1 teaspoon baking powder
- 1/2 tablespoon sugar
- 1/2 teaspoon salt, plus extra to taste
- 3/4 cup coarsely shredded cheddar cheese
- 1/2 cup minced fresh chives
- 1/2 cup chilled beer
- 1/2 tablespoon vegetable oil
- 1/2 egg
- 1 teaspoon Dijon mustard

Directions:

1. Sieve together the flour, salt and baking powder together in a large mixing bowl.
2. Add in the sugar and whisk well until well combined.
3. Add in the cheese and chives to the flour mixture and keep aside.
4. Pour the beer in a small mixing bowl.
5. Add the egg, salt and mustard to the beer and whisk until all the ingredients are well emulsified.
6. Slowly add the beer mixture to the prepared flour mixture and mix well until it forms a smooth dough. If you find the dough too dry, add in some more beer until it is moist.
7. Cover the dough loosely with a plastic wrap and refrigerate for about 35 to 40 minutes.
8. Lightly flour a flat work surface.
9. Transfer the chilled dough to the floured work surface and knead gently until the dough comes together.

10. Pat the dough to form a large 6-inch circle.
11. Slice the dough to get 4 wedges from it.
12. Lightly grease the 3-inch cooking rack with some butter or spray some cooking spray on it.
13. Arrange the beer scones on the greased rack.
14. Add the Extender Ring to the base.
15. Bake the beer scones at 350 degrees Fahrenheit for about 13 to 17 minutes or until the crust is golden.
16. Cool the scones on a cooling rack before serving.
17. Enjoy!

23. Corn, Jalapeno And Cheddar Muffins

Servings: Yields 6 muffins

Ingredients:

- 3/4 cup flour
- 1/2 cup sugar
- 3/4 cup cornmeal
- 1/2 teaspoon baking powder
- 1/2 teaspoon salt
- 1/4 teaspoon baking soda
- 1/3 cup sour cream
- 1/2 stick butter
- 1/3 cup milk
- 1 egg
- 1/2 onion, diced and caramelized
- 1/2 jalapeno, chopped and seeded
- 1/2 cup cheddar cheese, shredded

Directions:

1. Combine the flour, sugar, cornmeal, baking powder, salt and baking soda together in a large mixing bowl. Mix well until all the ingredients are well incorporated.
2. In another mixing bowl, pour in the sour cream, butter, milk and egg together. Whisk until all the ingredients are well emulsified.
3. Slowly add the flour mix into the sour cream mix, making sure that there are no lumps.
4. Add the caramelized onions, jalapenos and cheddar cheese to the batter and mix well.
5. Grease 6 muffin cups with some butter or spray them with some cooking spray.
6. Divide the batter among the 6 muffin cups.

7. Place the cups on the 3-inch cooking rack.
8. Bake the muffins at 350 degrees Fahrenheit for about 15 to 20 minutes or until a knife run through the center of the muffin comes out clean.
9. Cool the muffins on a wire rack before serving.
10. Enjoy!

Beef Recipes

24. Delicious Chuck Roast Beef With Roasted Potatoes, Onions & Carrots

Serving: Serves 2

Ingredients:

- 1/2 onion
- 3 baby gold potatoes
- 2 carrots, washed and peeled
- 1 tablespoon vegetable oil
- Freshly ground black pepper, to taste
- Salt, to taste
- 2 (1 pound) chuck roast
- 1 sprig rosemary
- 1 sprig thyme

Directions:

1. Coarsely chop the onion and carrots into bite sized pieces. Cut the potatoes into halves.

2. Place the carrots, onion and potatoes in a large mixing bowl.
3. Pour the oil over the vegetables and season to taste with salt and pepper. Toss well until combined. Keep aside.
4. Sprinkle the rosemary, thyme, salt and pepper over the chuck roasts. Rub the seasoning into the chuck roast using your fingers.
5. Place the chuck roasts and the oil coated vegetables on the 1-inch cooking rack.
6. Roast for about 30 to 35 minutes at 375 degrees Fahrenheit for medium rare doneness.
7. Once done to desired doneness, let the roast and veggies rest in the oven for another 5 minutes before transferring the chuck roast to a carving block.
8. Rest the meat for more 5 to 10 minutes before slicing.
9. Serve hot with the roasted vegetables on the side.
10. Enjoy!

25. Tangy Thai Steak, Bean Sprout And Peanut Salad

Serving: Serves 2

Ingredients:

Marinade Ingredients:

- 1/8 cup freshly squeezed lime juice
- 1/2 tablespoon soy sauce
- 1/8 cup rice wine vinegar
- 1/2 tablespoon sugar
- 1 1/2 tablespoons vegetable oil
- 1/4 teaspoon red pepper flakes

Salad Ingredients:

- 1 (1 pound) skirt steak
- Freshly ground black pepper, to taste
- Coarse salt, to taste
- 1/4 pound carrots, julienned
- 1/4 cup fresh mint leaves
- 1 small head romaine lettuce, cut crosswise into 1-inch ribbons
- 1/6 cup salted peanuts, chopped
- ½ cup fresh bean sprouts

Directions:

1. Pour the lemon juice, soy sauce, rice wine vinegar and vegetable oil together in the jar of a blender.
2. Add in the sugar and red pepper flakes and blitz until well combined.
3. Sprinkle salt and pepper over the skirt steak and rub it in using your fingers.
4. Place the seasoned steak in a baking dish.

5. Pour about ¼ of the prepared marinade over the steak. Turn the steak over repeatedly, until all the sides of the steak are well coated by the marinade.
6. Reserve the remaining marinade.
7. Cover the baking dish and refrigerate for about 2 to 4 hours.
8. Remove the steak from the marinade and shake off the excess marinade.
9. Place the steak on the 3-inch cooking rack and cook for 6 to 8 minutes on each side at 350 degrees Fahrenheit.
10. Once the steak is cooked to the desired degree of doneness, transfer the steak to the carving board and rest for about 5 to 10 minutes before slicing.
11. While the steak rests, place the carrots, sprouts, lettuce peanuts and mint together in a large mixing bowl.
12. Pour the reserved marinade over the prepared salad and toss well until all the ingredients are well coated.
13. Slice the steak into slices about ¼ inch thick against the grain and then cut the slices into halves in the opposite direction.
14. Spoon the prepared salad onto a serving plate and place the steak slices over the bed of salad. Sprinkle salt and pepper over the steak slices and serve immediately.
15. Enjoy!

26. Steak Sandwiches

Serving: Serves 2

Ingredients:

- 1 (6 ounce) top sirloin steak
- Salt, to taste
- 2 1/2 tablespoons olive oil, divided
- Freshly ground black pepper, to taste
- 1/4 cup mayonnaise
- 2 French rolls
- 1 tablespoons parsley
- ½ tablespoon garlic

Directions:

1. Pour about 1-½ tablespoons of the olive oil over the steak and rub the oil on both sides of the steak.
2. Sprinkle the salt and pepper over both the sides of the steak and rub the seasoning into the steak using your fingers.
3. Place the prepared steak on the 4-inch cooking rack and place it in your NuWave oven.
4. Cook for about 6 minutes per side on the HI power setting.
5. Remove the steak from the oven and keep it aside to cool.
6. Cut open the buns and place them on the 4-inch cooking rack.
7. Toast on the HI power setting for about 4 minutes.
8. While the buns are toasting, mix together the mayonnaise, parsley, garlic and the remaining 1-tablespoon olive oil in the jar of a blender. Blitz until all the ingredients emulsify together.

9. Once the steak is well rested, slice it into ¼ inch slices against the grain.
10. Spread the prepared garlic mayonnaise over the toasted bottom buns and place the steak slices over it.
11. Cover with the toasted top buns.
12. Serve immediately with a side of fresh French fries or a fresh salad.
13. Enjoy!

27. Halloween Style Jack O' Peppers

Serving: Serves 3

Ingredients:

- 3 bell peppers
- 1/4 pound ground beef
- 1 cup wild rice, cooked
- 1/8 cup Italian sausage
- 1/4 cup mushrooms, diced
- 1/2 onion, diced
- 1 tablespoon garlic, minced
- Freshly ground black pepper, to taste
- Salt, to taste

Directions:

1. Use a sharp knife to carve a jack o' lantern face in the pepper. Slice the top of the pepper and reserve the tops for later.
2. Place the ground beef, wild rice, Italian sausage, mushrooms, onion, garlic, salt and pepper together in a large mixing bowl. Mix well until well combined.
3. Spoon the prepared stuffing into the carved peppers until the jack o' lantern face is completely filled through.
4. Place the peppers on the 3-inch cooking rack.
5. Bake for about 15 to 20 minutes at 350 degrees Fahrenheit.
6. Once the timer is up, place the reserved tops over the peppers.
7. Continue baking at 350 degrees Fahrenheit for another 7 to 10 minutes.
8. Transfer the peppers to the serving dish.
9. Serve hot.
10. Enjoy!

28. Cheesy Meatloaf

Serving: Serves 2

Ingredients:

- 1/2 cup carrots, diced
- 1/2 pound ground chuck
- 1/2 cup onion, diced
- 1/2 cup Italian-seasoned bread crumbs
- 1 teaspoon salt
- 1 egg
- 1/2 teaspoon ground pepper
- 1 tablespoon garlic, minced
- 1/4 cup ketchup
- Shredded cheese (optional)
- 2 slices provolone cheese, cut into strips

Directions:

1. Heat a pan on a medium high flame and add the carrots and onions to it. Cook until the veggies soften.
2. Place the softened carrots and onions, ground beef, egg, pepper, breadcrumbs, salt and garlic together in the bowl of a stand mixer.
3. Mix on the mixer's lowest speed until all the ingredients are properly incorporated.
4. Spray a meat loaf pan with some non-stick cooking spray or grease it with some butter.
5. Pour the meatloaf mix from the bowl into the greased pan. Cover with a cling wrap and refrigerate for an hour.
6. Remove the meatloaf from the pan directly on to the 3-inch cooking rack.
7. Cook for about 20 to 25 minutes at 350 degrees Fahrenheit.

8. Carefully open the dome of your NuWave oven and pour the ketchup over the meatloaf.
9. Cover the ketchup covered meatloaf with slices of the provolone slices and top with the remaining shredded cheese.
10. Continue cooking at 350 degrees Fahrenheit for another 10 to 15 minutes or until the cheese gets a nice brown hue.
11. Serve hot with a side of your favorite condiment.
12. Enjoy!

29. Corned Beef And Brown Rice Stuffed Cabbage Rolls

Serving: Serves 1

Ingredients:

- 1/2 pound cooked corned beef, chopped
- 1 1/2 celery stalks, finely chopped
- 1/2 cup cooked brown rice
- 1/2 onion, finely chopped
- 1/2 head green cabbage, blanched
- 1 egg, lightly beaten
- 1/2 cup beef broth
- Freshly ground black pepper, to taste
- Kosher salt, to taste

Directions:

1. Place the cooked corned beef and the cooked brown rice together in a large mixing bowl. Mix well until well combined.
2. Add the celery, egg and onion to the mixing bowl. Mix well until well combined.
3. Sprinkle salt and pepper over the beef mixture and mix well.
4. Lay the cabbage leaves on a flat surface and place about 3 tablespoons of the prepared corned beef mixture on each leaf.
5. Roll the leaf up, tucking in the sides as you go.
6. Place the prepared cabbage rolls directly onto the liner pan with the seam side down.
7. Pour the beef broth onto the rolls.
8. Cover the liner pan with some aluminum foil and bake on the HI power setting for about 20 to 25 minutes.
9. Serve hot with the condiment of your choice.
10. Enjoy!

30. Crabmeat Stuffed Beef Roulade With A Buttery Port Wine Sauce

Serving: Serves 1

Ingredients:

Roulade Ingredients:

- 1 tablespoon butter
- 4 ounces crimini mushrooms, sliced
- 1 tablespoon shallots, minced
- 1 tablespoon olive oil
- 1/4 pound lump crabmeat, carefully picked over and cartilage removed
- 1/8 cup parsley, minced
- 1/8 cup white wine
- Pinch kosher salt
- 1/4 pound fresh spinach, washed and stems removed
- 1/2 pound bottom or top round, trimmed and butterflied to ½ inch thickness
- Pinch white pepper

Sauce Ingredients:

- 1/2 cup port wine
- Pinch of salt
- 1 tablespoon unsalted butter
- Pinch of pepper

Directions:

Roulade Directions:

1. Place the butter and olive oil in a large skillet and heat over a medium high flame until the butter has melted and combined with the oil.

2. Add the shallots and onions to the pan and sauté for about 3 to 5 minutes or until the vegetables have softened.
3. Pour the port wine into the pan and cook for another 2 to 3 minutes or until the port wine has completely evaporated.
4. Add the parsley, crabmeat and spinach to the pan and cook for about 4 to 5 minutes or until the edges of the spinach have wilted.
5. Season to taste with salt and pepper and remove the pan off the flame. Let the mix cool to room temperature.
6. Place the beef on a flat work surface and sprinkle salt and pepper over the beef.
7. Lightly squeeze the crabmeat mixture and remove the extra water from it.
8. Place the crabmeat mixture on the seasoned loin and spread the mixture down the center of the loin, leaving about ½ an inch border from around the edges.
9. Start rolling the loin over the crabmeat from the short end tightly.
10. Tie the roll with a kitchen twine at regular 1-inch intervals.
11. Sprinkle salt and white pepper around the outside of the roulade and place the roulade with its seam side down on the 4-inch cooking rack.
12. Roast the roulade on the HI power setting for about 5 to 6 minutes per side and meat is well browned. The internal temperature of the meat should reach 150 degrees Fahrenheit.
13. Remove the roulade from the oven and place on a cutting board, loosely covered with a kitchen towel.

Let the roulade rest for about 6 to 7 minutes before slicing it.

14. Slice the roulade into 3/4-inch thick slices and serve hot covered with the prepared port wine sauce.
15. Enjoy!

Sauce Directions:

1. In a small stockpot, pour the port wine and heat on a high flame until the port wine is bubbling.
2. Once the port wine is bubbling, reduce the heat so that the port wine is simmering.
3. Simmer until the port wine is reduced to about 1/6 cup.
4. Remove the wine from the heat and add in the butter.
5. Whisk well until well combined.
6. Season to taste with salt and pepper.
7. Keep warm while the roulade cooks.

31. NuWave Style Bacon, Liver & Onions

Serving: Serves 2

Ingredients:

- 1/2 pound calf liver, 1/2-inch thick
- 1/4 teaspoon salt
- 1/4 cup milk
- 1/4 teaspoon pepper
- 1 medium onion, sliced in to thick rings
- 1/4 teaspoon seasoned salt
- 3 - 4 slices of bacon, cut in half

Directions:

1. Place the liver in a mixing bowl.
2. Add in the milk, pepper, seasoned salt and salt and mix well until all the sides are well coated.
3. Cover and let it rest for an hour.
4. Place the onion rings on the 3-inch cooking rack.
5. Drain the liver from the marinade and shake off the excess marinade. Place the liver on the onion slices.
6. Place the bacon slices on the liver.
7. Cook for about 8 minutes at 350 degrees Fahrenheit.
8. Remove the bacon slices from the liver and flip the liver over. Return the bacon slices and continue cooking at the same temperature for another 8 to 10 minutes.
9. Once done cooking, let the liver rest in the oven (with the dome on) for another 5 to 7 minutes).
10. Serve hot with the bacon and onions.
11. Enjoy!

32. Easy Rib Eye Steak With Parmesan Topped Sweet Potatoes

Serving: Serves 1

Ingredients:

Steak Ingredients:

- 1 (12-ounce) rib eye steak
- 1/8 teaspoon kosher salt
- 1/8 teaspoon black pepper
- 1/4 tablespoon extra-virgin olive oil

Sweet Potatoes Ingredients:

- 1 large sweet potato
- 1/2 tablespoon extra-virgin olive oil
- 1 clove garlic, minced
- 1 tablespoon parmesan cheese, grated
- 1/8 teaspoon black pepper
- 1/8 teaspoon kosher salt

Directions:

Steak Directions:

1. Pat the steak lightly with a kitchen towel, until the steak is dry to touch.
2. Sprinkle the salt and pepper over both sides of the steak and rub the seasonings into the meat using your fingers.
3. Pour the olive oil over the steak and rub well.
4. Place the steak on the 1-inch cooking rack.
5. Roast on the HI power setting for about 6 to 7 minutes for medium rare doneness, 8 to 10 minutes for medium doneness and 11 to 13 minutes for a well-done steak.

6. Once done to your desired level of doneness, allow the meat to rest for about 8 to 10 minutes, covered loosely with a piece of foil.

Sweet Potatoes Directions:

1. Cut the potatoes into quarters for 4 equal sized wedges.
2. Place the potato wedges in a large mixing bowl and add in the olive oil, garlic, salt and pepper.
3. Toss well to coat the potatoes evenly.
4. Cover the 1-inch cooking rack with a foil and spray it with some cooking spray.
5. Place the oil tossed potato wedges on the foil with their skin sides down.
6. Cook on the HI power setting for about 18 to 20 minutes or until the potatoes are tender and become well browned.
7. Sprinkle the Parmesan over the potato wedges and serve with the steak immediately.
8. Enjoy!

Poultry Recipes

33. Cheese Topped Turkey Burgers

Serving: Serves 1

Ingredients:

- 1/2 pound ground turkey
- 1/2 garlic clove, finely minced
- 1/2 lemon, zested and juiced
- 1 scallion or green onion, finely sliced
- 1/2 teaspoon black pepper
- 1/2 egg, lightly beaten
- 1/2 teaspoon kosher salt
- 1/4 cup Japanese Panko breadcrumbs
- 1/2 tablespoon extra-virgin olive oil
- 2 whole grain buns
- 1 (6 ounce) goat cheese log, cut into 1/2-inch slices

Directions:

1. Place the turkey, lemon juice, scallions, salt, olive oil, lemon zest, garlic, egg, pepper and breadcrumbs together in a large mixing bowl.
2. Mix well until all the ingredients are well incorporated.
3. Divide the turkey mixture into two equal halves.
4. Form each half into a patty that is about 1-inch thick.
5. Set the patties aside and let the meat rest.
6. Slice the buns into two halves and place all 4 pieces on the 1-inch cooking rack.
7. Cook on the HI power setting for about 5 to 6 minutes or until the buns are well toasted.
8. Remove the toasted buns from the oven and keep aside.
9. Cover the cooking rack with a foil and spray the foil with some cooking spray.
10. Place the prepared turkey patties on the foil.
11. Cook on the HI power setting for about 8 minutes.
12. Turn the patties over and continue cooking on the HI power setting for another 4 minutes.
13. Divide the goat cheese into two equal portions and sprinkle it over the patties.
14. Continue cooking on the HI setting for another 4 minutes or until the cheese is melted enough to spread.
15. Place the turkey patties with their cheese side up on the toasted bun bottom.
16. Top with the top bun.
17. Serve hot with a side of freshly fried French fries.
18. Enjoy!

34. Cheese Stuffed Turkey Burgers With A Sun Dried Tomato Mayonnaise

Serving: Serves 2

Ingredients:

Burger Ingredients:

- 1/2 large shallot, finely chopped (1/8 cup)
- 1/4 teaspoon salt
- 1 tablespoon olive oil
- 1/8 teaspoon black pepper
- 2 1/2 ounces extra-sharp cheddar cheese, cut into 2 slices
- 3/4 pounds ground turkey
- 2 hamburger buns or Kaiser rolls
- Lettuce leaves

Sun Dried Tomato Mayonnaise Ingredients:

- 1/8 cup oil packed sun dried tomatoes, drained
- 1 teaspoon cider vinegar
- 1/2 tablespoon water
- 1/8 cup mayonnaise
- 1/8 teaspoon salt

Directions:

1. Place the sun-dried tomatoes, cider vinegar, water, mayonnaise and salt together in the jar of a blender and blitz until well emulsified.
2. Empty the sun dried tomato mayonnaise in a small bowl and cover with a cling wrap. Refrigerate until the burgers are ready.
3. Place the shallots in a small baking dish and place it on the 4-inch cooking rack.

4. Cook the shallots on the HI power setting for about 3 to 5 minutes.
5. Once done, transfer the shallots to a small bowl and season to taste with salt and pepper.
6. Add the shallots to the turkey and mix well until combined.
7. Divide the turkey mix into 4 equal halves and place on a sheet of wax paper.
8. Pat each quarter until about 1/2 inch thick.
9. Cover two patties with 1 piece of cheese each.
10. Top the cheese covered patties with the leftover patties.
11. Lightly pinch the edges of the two patties so that the cheese is completely sealed inside the meat. This will make you 2 stuffed patties.
12. Place the prepared stuffed patties on the 4-inch cooking rack and cook on the HI power setting for about 7 to 8 minutes on each side or until the internal temperature of the meat reaches about 150 degrees.
13. Slice the burger buns or roll into two halves and toast the buns on the 4-inch cooking rack with their sliced side up for about 4 minutes.
14. Place the toasted bun halves on a serving plate, spread the prepared sun dried tomato mayonnaise on it, place the stuffed patty and top with the top half of the toasted bun.
15. Serve hot with a side of a fresh salad.
16. Enjoy!

35. Tangy Cilantro And Lime Chicken

Serving: Serves 6

Ingredients:

- 2 tablespoon honey
- 4 cloves garlic
- 1/2 teaspoon oregano
- 1/2 teaspoon black pepper
- 1/2 cup red onion
- 1 teaspoon salt
- 8 limes, juiced
- 1 cup fresh cilantro
- 2/3 cup canola oil
- 6 (6-ounce) chicken breasts

Directions:

1. In the jar of the blender, add honey, garlic, oregano, black pepper, red onion, salt, lime juice, cilantro and canola oil together.
2. Blitz until the mix is well emulsified.
3. Place the chicken breasts in a large sealable bag and pour the marinade into the bag.
4. Seal the bag and toss well until the chicken pieces are well coated in the marinade.
5. Refrigerate the marinated chicken overnight.
6. Remove the chicken breast from the marinade and shake of the excess marinade. Reserve the extra marinade.
7. Place the chicken breasts on the 3-inch cooking rack and cook for about 11 to 13 minutes at 350 degrees Fahrenheit.
8. Turn the chicken breasts over and brush the remaining marinade over them.

9. Continue cooking at 350 degrees Fahrenheit for another 11 to 13 minutes.
10. Remove the chicken breasts from the oven and rest for a few minutes before slicing.
11. Serve hot with the condiment of your choice.
12. Enjoy!

36. Delicious Chicken Wraps With Onions And Bell Peppers

Serving: Serves 2

Ingredients:

- 1 tablespoon olive oil
- 1/2 onion, julienned
- 4 raw chicken tenders, sliced in half
- 1/4 teaspoon salt
- 1/4 teaspoon cumin
- 1/4 teaspoon pepper
- 1/4 teaspoon paprika
- 1/2 yellow bell pepper, julienned
- 1/4 teaspoon garlic powder
- 1/2 orange bell pepper, julienned
- 2 flour tortillas
- 1/2 red bell pepper, julienned

Directions:

1. Pour the olive oil into the liner pan of the NuWave oven.
2. Place the chicken tenders and onions in the liner pan.
3. Sprinkle the salt, cumin, garlic, pepper and paprika over the chicken tenders and onions.
4. Cook the chicken and onions at 400 degrees Fahrenheit for about 5 to 7 minutes.
5. Add the yellow bell pepper and orange bell pepper into the liner pan and mix well.
6. Cook for another 5 to 7 minutes at 400 degrees Fahrenheit.
7. Place the tortillas on a flat working surface.
8. Spoon the prepared chicken and vegetable mix over the tortillas.

9. Roll into a tight roll.
10. Slice at an angle and serve immediately with the condiments of your choice.
11. Enjoy!

37. Italian Spice Rubbed Turkey

Serving: Serves 3 - 4

Ingredients:

- 1 (5 to 8 pound) turkey
- 1 tablespoon dry rub
- 1 tablespoon Italian seasoning
- Salt, to taste
- 1/8 cup olive oil
- Freshly ground black pepper, to taste

Directions:

1. Combine the dry rub and Italian seasoning together in a small mixing bowl.
2. Pour the olive oil over the turkey and pour the prepared seasoning over it.
3. Rub the seasoning into the turkey meat.
4. Place the spice rubbed turkey with on the 11-inch cooking rack with its breast side down.
5. Add the Extender Ring to the base tray if required.
6. Cook for about 12 minutes per pound, pausing around the halfway mark to flip the turkey over at 375 degrees Fahrenheit.
7. Serve hot.
8. Enjoy!

38. Fresh Turkey, Lettuce And Blue Cheese Salad

Serving: Serves 2

Ingredients:

- 2 slices bacon, thick cut
- 1/2 large head romaine lettuce
- 2 eggs
- 1/8 cup olive oil
- 1/2 teaspoon Dijon mustard
- 1 1/2 tablespoons red-wine vinegar
- 4 ounces roasted turkey breast, cut into cubes
- 1 1/2 ounces blue cheese, crumbled
- 1/2 ripe avocado, pitted, peeled and diced
- 2 plum tomatoes cut into ½ inch dice
- Freshly ground black pepper, to taste
- Salt, to taste

Directions:

1. Place the eggs on the liner pan on one side of the pan.
2. Place the 4-inch cooking rack on the liner pan. Place the bacon pieces on the side on the opposite side of the eggs.
3. Cook on the HI power setting for about 13 to 15 minutes.
4. While the eggs and bacon are cooking arrange the lettuce leaves on top of each other and roll to form a cylinder.
5. Hold the lettuce cylinder tightly and slice into ¼ inch strips.
6. Place the lettuce strips in a large mixing bowl and season to taste with salt and pepper.

7. Once the eggs and bacon are done, drain the bacon on a paper towel and remove the cooking rack. Be careful, as the cooking rack will be extremely hot.
8. Use oven mitts or oven tongs to transfer the eggs under a stream of cold water or place them in an ice bath.
9. Peel the eggs and set aside until completely cooled.
10. Once the eggs have cooled, chop the drained bacon and eggs into small pieces and keep aside.
11. In a small mixing bowl, whisk together the vinegar, salt, oil, pepper and mustard together. Whisk until all the ingredients are well incorporated.
12. Pour about half of the prepared dressing over the chopped lettuce and toss well until well coated.
13. Place the dressing covered lettuce onto a serving dish.
14. Add the diced bacon, turkey, blue cheese, eggs, avocado and tomatoes over the lettuce, placing each ingredient in one separate section.
15. Season to taste with salt and pepper and pour the remaining dressing over the salad.
16. Serve immediately.
17. Enjoy!

39. Dijon And Garlic Roasted Chicken And Onions

Serving: Serves 2

Ingredients:

- 2 chicken breasts, bone in, skin on
- 1/2 tablespoon olive oil
- 1 tablespoon Dijon mustard
- 1/4 yellow onion, sliced
- 2 sprigs parsley leaves, chopped
- 1/4 cup low sodium chicken stock
- 1 teaspoon garlic, chopped
- 1/2 teaspoon red chili flakes
- 1/2 teaspoon sugar
- 1/2 teaspoon black pepper
- 1 teaspoon salt

Directions:

1. Combine the olive oil, Dijon mustard, parsley leaves, low sodium chicken stock, garlic, red chili flakes, sugar, black pepper and salt together in a large mixing bowl. Whisk well until well combined.
2. Once the ingredients are emulsified, add the onion and chicken to the bowl.
3. Toss the chicken and onion well until they are completely coated with the marinade.
4. Cover the bowl with some cling wrap.
5. Refrigerate the chicken for about an hour or two.
6. Place the chicken with its skin side down on the 4-inch cooking rack.
7. Cook on the HI power setting for about 8 to 10 minutes on each side.

8. Once the chicken is done, rest it for about 5 minutes before slicing.
9. Serve over a bed of wild rice or roasted sweet potatoes.
10. Enjoy!

40. Roasted Chicken In A Homemade BBQ Sauce

Serving: Serves 2

Ingredients:

- 1/2 teaspoon hot sauce
- 1/4 cup light brown sugar
- 1/6 cup cider vinegar
- 1 1/2 tablespoons Dijon mustard
- 1/8 cup molasses
- 1/4 cup ketchup
- 2 garlic cloves, minced
- 1 whole (1 ½ pound) chicken, cut into individual pieces
- Salt, to taste
- 1/2 tablespoon olive oil
- Freshly ground black pepper to taste

Directions:

1. Combine together the hot sauce, cider vinegar, brown sugar, molasses, Dijon mustard, garlic cloves and ketchup together in an oven safe baking dish.
2. Place the baking dish on the 1-inch cooking rack and cook on the HI power setting for about 8 to 10 minutes.
3. Place the chicken pieces in a large mixing bowl. Pour the olive oil over the pieces and toss well to coat.
4. Pour some barbeque sauce over the oil coated chicken – just enough to coat.
5. Toss well until the chicken is well coated in the sauce.
6. Spray cooking spray over the 4-inch cooking rack.

7. Place the barbeque sauce covered chicken pieces on the rack, with their skin side down and cook on the HI power setting for about 10 to 12 minutes.
8. Remove the chicken from the oven and brush with the remaining barbeque sauce.
9. Return the chicken pieces to the oven, this time skin side up.
10. Continue cooking on the HI power setting for another 10 to 12 minutes or until the internal temperature of the chicken reads about 165 degrees Fahrenheit.
11. Serve hot with a fresh salad on the side.
12. Enjoy!

41. Wild Rice Stuffed Roasted Chicken Breast

Serving: Serves 1

Ingredients:

- 1 (6 to 8 ounce) chicken breast (with wing bone attached)
- 1 cup cooled wild rice
- 2 cups water
- 1/8 cup green pumpkin seeds
- 1/8 teaspoon ground cumin
- 1/8 cup dried golden raisins
- Freshly ground black pepper, to taste
- Salt, to taste

Directions:

1. Extract the tenderloin from the chicken breast.
2. Dice the tenderloin into bite sized pieces and set aside.
3. Pour water into a 1 and half-quart saucepan and heat over a high flame, uncovered, until the water is boiling.
4. Add the wild rice into the water and stir well.
5. Reduce the flame to a medium low and simmer the rice for about an hour or until the rice is tender to touch.
6. Add the pumpkin seeds, cumin, pepper, raisins, salt and diced tenderloin to the rice and mix well.
7. Carefully cut a pocket into the chicken breast and spoon the prepared rice mixture into it.
8. Pour the olive oil over the stuffed chicken breast.

9. Place the stuffed chicken on a 3-inch cooking rack and roast the chicken for about 20 minutes on each side at 375 degrees Fahrenheit.
10. Heat the juices from the pan until well reduced.
11. Pour the reduced juices over the chicken and serve immediately.
12. Enjoy!

42. Thai Style Chicken With Assorted Vegetables

Serving: Serves 2

Ingredients:

- 2 boneless, skinless chicken breasts
- 1/4 teaspoon red pepper flakes
- 6 tablespoons Thai sauce
- 1/2 cup zucchini
- 6 strips red or yellow pepper
- 1 cup yellow squash
- 1 teaspoon olive oil
- Pepper, to taste
- Salt, to taste

Directions:

1. Place the chicken breasts on the 1-inch or the 4-inch cooking rack.
2. In a small mixing bowl, combine together the red pepper flakes and the Thai sauce.
3. Spoon about half the prepared sauce over the chicken breasts.
4. Cook the chicken for about 8 to 9 minutes on HI power. (Increase the cooking time to 10 minutes if you are using frozen chicken.)
5. Place all the vegetables in a large sealable bag and add in the salt, pepper and olive oil. Seal the bag and toss until well coated.
6. Once the chicken is done, flip it over and spread the remaining sauce over the breast.
7. Place the oil-coated vegetables around the chicken breasts and continue cooking on the HI power for another 8 to 10 minutes.

8. Serve hot.
9. Enjoy!

43. Cheesy Chicken Nugget Casserole

Serving: Serves 2

Ingredients:

- 1/2 (13-1/2 ounce) package frozen chicken nuggets
- 1/2 (26 1/2 ounce) can spaghetti sauce
- 3 tablespoons grated Parmesan cheese
- 1/2 teaspoon Italian seasoning
- 1/2 cup shredded Mozzarella cheese

Directions:

1. Grease an 8-inch by 8-inch baking dish with some butter.
2. Place the chicken nuggets in the greased baking dish in a single layer.
3. Sprinkle a layer of the Parmesan cheese over it.
4. Pour the spaghetti sauce over the Parmesan.
5. Top with the mozzarella cheese and Italian seasoning.
6. Place the baking dish on the 1-inch cooking rack and cook on the HI power setting for about 10 minutes.
7. Cover the baking dish with a foil and continue cooking for another 5 minutes.
8. Serve hot.
9. Enjoy!

Pork Recipes

44. Anise & Fennel Rubbed Roasted Pork Loin

Serving: Serves 4

Ingredients:

- Kosher salt, to taste
- 1 tablespoon fennel seeds, crushed
- Freshly ground pepper, to taste
- 1/2 tablespoon anise seeds, crushed
- 1/2 tablespoon olive oil
- 1/2 teaspoon crushed red pepper flakes
- 1 (3/4 pound) pork loin

Directions:

1. Combine the black pepper, anise seeds, fennel seeds and red pepper flakes together in a small mixing bowl.
2. Pour in the olive oil and mix well.

3. Place the pork loin in a dish and pour the marinade over it.
4. Cover the dish with a cling wrap and refrigerate for about 4 to 5 hours.
5. Place the marinated pork loin on the 3-inch cooking rack.
6. Cook the pork loin for about 11 to 13 minutes on each side at 350 degrees Fahrenheit.
7. Transfer the pork to a carving board and rest for about 5 to 10 minutes before slicing.
8. Serve hot.
9. Enjoy!

45. Zesty Orange Holiday Ham

Serving: Serves 3 - 4

Ingredients:

- 1 (2 - 4 pound) ham
- 1/2 tablespoon red pepper flakes
- 1/2 teaspoon sage
- 1 tablespoon salt
- Zest from 1/2 orange
- Black pepper, to taste
- 1/2 cup orange juice

Directions:

1. Combine together the red pepper flakes, sage, salt, orange zest and black pepper together in a small mixing bowl.
2. Pour the prepared spice mix into the orange juice and mix well until combined.
3. Pour the prepared marinade over the ham and turn it around until all the sides are well coated.
4. Refrigerate covered for a few hours.
5. Place the Extender Ring on the base if required and place the marinated ham on the 1-inch cooking rack.
6. Cook the ham for about 15 minutes per pound at 350degrees Fahrenheit. Make sure you turn the ham over around the halfway mark.
7. Transfer the ham to a carving board and rest for about 5 to 10 minutes before slicing.
8. Serve hot.
9. Enjoy!

46. Chorizo And Beef Burgers

Serving: Serves 2

Ingredients:

- 1/4 pound fresh chorizo, casings removed
- 1/2 teaspoon ground cumin
- 1/4 pound lean ground beef
- 1/4 teaspoon ground coriander
- 1 clove garlic, finely chopped
- 1 tablespoon cilantro, finely chopped and divided
- Kosher salt, to taste
- 1/4 cup mayonnaise
- Freshly ground black pepper, to taste
- 3/4 tablespoons hot sauce
- 1 tablespoon olive oil
- 1/2 teaspoon fresh lime juice
- 2 slices pepper jack cheese
- Lettuce leaves
- 2 hamburger buns, lightly toasted,
- 1/2 ripe Hass avocado, pitted, peeled, and thinly sliced
- Sliced tomatoes,

Directions:

1. Combine the chorizo, cumin, ½ tablespoon cilantro, salt, beef, coriander, garlic and pepper together in a medium sized mixing bowl.
2. Divide the mixture into two equal parts and make patties that are 3-inches wide and 1-inch thick.
3. Place the prepared patties on the 4-inch cooking rack and cook for about 7 to 8 minutes on the HI power setting.

4. While the patties are cooking, combine together the remaining cilantro, hot sauce, salt, mayonnaise, lime juice, and pepper together in a small mixing bowl.
5. Place a single slice of cheese over both the patties and cook for another minute on the HI power setting or until the cheese melts.
6. Spread he prepared mayonnaise and hot sauce mix over the bun.
7. Add the lettuce, avocado and tomato over it.
8. Top with the cheese covered patties.
9. Serve immediately.
10. Enjoy!

47. Chorizo And Shrimp Stuffed Chilies With A Black Bean Salsa And Avocado Cream

Serving: Serves 2

Ingredients:

- 1 ear fresh corn
- 1/2 bunch green onions, chopped
- 1/2 can black beans, rinsed
- 1/2 jalapeno, minced
- 1/2 teaspoon garlic, minced
- 1/2 red pepper, minced
- 1/2 small bunch cilantro, chopped
- Olive oil to taste
- 1/2 lime, juiced
- Pepper, to taste
- Salt, to taste

- 6 small oval yellow or red peppers
- 1 cup small shrimp
- 1 cup chorizo
- 1/2 cup Chihuahua cheese

- 1/4 cup sour cream
- 1 ripe avocado

Directions:

1. Place the ear of corn on the 3-inch cooking rack and roast for about 5 minutes per side at 350 degrees Fahrenheit.
2. Once done, use a sharp knife to remove the corn from the cob.

3. Combine the roasted corn kernels, onions, red pepper, cilantro, beans, jalapenos, garlic and lime together in a mixing bowl.

4. Pour the olive oil over the prepared salsa and season to taste with salt and pepper. Keep aside.

5. Remove the top 1/3 of the chili, remove the seeds and slice the chilies lengthwise.

6. Combine the chorizo and shrimp together and spoon it into the chilies.

7. Place the stuffed chilies on the 3-inch cooking rack and cook for about 12 to 15 minutes at 350 degrees Fahrenheit.

8. Add the cheese over the chilies and continue baking until the cheese is melted and well browned.

9. While the chilies roast, remove the flesh from the avocados and add the sour cream to it.

10. Mix well until well combined. Set aside.

11. Spoon the prepared salsa on a serving plate and places the stuffed chilies on it. Spoon the avocado sour cream over the chilies and serve immediately.

12. Enjoy!

48. Roasted Pork Chops In A Sweet And Sour Sauce

Serving: Serves 1

Ingredients:

Pork Ingredients:

- 1 center cut bone in pork chop
- Freshly cracked black pepper, to taste
- Kosher salt, to taste
- 1/8 teaspoon extra virgin olive oil

Sauce Ingredients:

- 3 tablespoons leeks, julienne cut
- 1/2 tablespoon extra-virgin olive oil
- 1/2 red bell pepper
- Freshly cracked black pepper, to taste
- 1/2 tablespoon rosemary, divided
- 1/2 small red onion, sliced
- 1 1/2 tablespoons raisins
- 3 tablespoons balsamic vinegar
- 2 tablespoons honey
- 1/2 cup beef stock
- 3 cherry tomatoes, sliced in half
- 1 1/2 tablespoons pine nuts
- ½ tablespoon butter

Directions:

Pork Directions:

1. Sprinkle salt and pepper on both sides of the pork chop.

2. Pour the olive oil over the pork chop and rub it in using your fingers.
3. Place the pork chop on the 4-inch cooking rack.
4. Roast for about 5 to 7 minutes per side on the HI power setting.
5. While the pork roasts, prepare the sauce.
6. Rest the pork for about 10 to 15 minutes before serving.

Sauce Directions:

1. Heat a medium sized frying pan over a medium flame.
2. Add in the bell peppers and leeks and cook until they are well caramelized.
3. Pour in the oil and add in the black pepper. Toss well.
4. Add in the onions and increase the flame to high.
5. Once the onions have softened add in ¼ tablespoon rosemary and cook for another minute.
6. Once the rosemary is aromatic, add in the raisins.
7. Pour in the honey and mix well. Heat until the mixture is bubbling.
8. Add in the balsamic vinegar and continue heating until the sauce coats the back of a spoon.
9. Add in the beef stock and continue heating until the sauce thickens and reduces to half its original quantity.
10. Just before you serve, add in the pine nuts and the remaining rosemary.
11. Add in the butter and tomatoes and mix lightly.
12. Pour over the pork chops and serve immediately.
13. Enjoy!

49. Pork Roast with Honey Mustard Glaze

Serving: Serves 3

Ingredients:

- 1 (1 1/2 pound) boneless center cut pork roast, untied
- 1 tablespoon honey
- 1 tablespoon white wine vinegar
- 1 tablespoon Dijon mustard
- 1/2 tablespoon parsley, roughly chopped
- 1/2 tablespoon grain or Pommery mustard
- 1/2 tablespoon extra-virgin olive oil
- Freshly ground black pepper, to taste
- Kosher salt, to taste

Directions:

1. Combine together the honey, white wine vinegar, Dijon mustard, parsley, Pommery mustard, olive oil, black pepper and salt together in a small mixing bowl. Keep aside.
2. Place the pork roast of a flat working surface.
3. Sprinkle salt, olive oil and black pepper over, turning it around to ensure all its sides get coated.
4. Place the pork on the 1-inch cooking rack and pour the prepared glaze over it.
5. Cook for about 45 minutes on the HI power setting or until the internal temperature of the pork roast reads 155 degrees Fahrenheit.
6. Rest the pork for about 10 minutes before slicing.
7. Serve hot.
8. Enjoy!

50. Healthy Ham And Cheese Sandwiches

Serving: Serves 2

Ingredients:

- 4 tablespoons Dijon mustard, divided
- 4 slices 7 Grain bread
- 6 - 8 ounces baked ham, thinly sliced and divided
- 9 - 10 slices Gruyere cheese, divided

Directions:

1. Spread about 1 tablespoon of the mustard on each slice of bread.
2. Place the bread slices, mustard side up, on the 4-inch cooking rack.
3. Cover two slices with 2 slices of cheese each and the remaining two slices with ham.
4. Cook on the HI power setting for about 5 minutes or until the cheese has completely melted.
5. Assemble the sandwiches and top with the remaining cheese.
6. Cook for another 3 to 4 minutes or until the cheese melts.
7. Serve hot.
8. Enjoy!

51. Quick BBQ Pork Chops With Roasted Vegetables

Serving: Serves 6

Ingredients:

- 6 pork medallions or boneless chops (4-ounce)
- 2 teaspoons soy sauce
- 6 tablespoons BBQ sauce

Vegetables

- 1/2 cup sliced zucchini
- 1/2 sliced onion
- 1/2 cup sliced yellow squash
- 10 cherry tomatoes
- 2 sprigs rosemary, whole
- Salt, to taste
- 2 teaspoons olive oil
- Freshly ground black pepper, to taste

Directions:

1. Place the pork medallions on the 1-inch cooking rack.
2. In a mixing bowl, combine together the soya sauce and BBQ sauce.
3. Pour about half the sauce over the medallions and roast on the HI setting for about 4 to 5 minutes.
4. While the pork roasts, place the zucchini, onion, yellow squash, and tomatoes together in a large sealable bag.
5. Add in the rosemary, salt, olive oil and pepper and toss well until well coated.
6. When the pork is done, flip it over and arrange all the vegetables around it.

7. Pour the remaining sauce over the pork and vegetables and cook on the HI setting for about 8 minutes.
8. Rest the pork for about 10 minutes before slicing.
9. Serve hot with the roasted vegetables.
10. Enjoy!

52. Tangy Orange And Mustard Glazed Ham

Serving: Serves 5 - 6

Ingredients:

- 1 (5 pound) cooked bone-in ham
- 1/2 cup hot water
- 1/2 large orange
- 3 whole cloves
- 1/2 tablespoon French brown mustard
- 6 tablespoons light brown sugar
- 1/4 cup honey
- 1 tablespoon Grand Marnier
- 1 teaspoon soy sauce

Directions:

1. Using a sharp knife, score the fat of the ham in a diamond pattern.
2. Juice the orange and pour it over the ham.
3. Remove the zest of the orange, making sure you do not zest the white part too.
4. Pour the zest over the orange juice covered ham.
5. If required, add the Extender Ring to the base of your oven.
6. Place the orange covered ham on the 1-inch cooking rack.
7. Pour the water into the liner pan and add the cloves to it.
8. Roast the ham on the 8 power setting for about 14 to 16 minutes per pound of meat.
9. While the ham is roasting, combine the brown sugar, honey, Grand Marnier, mustard and soy sauce together in a small mixing bowl. Whisk until well combined.

10. When the ham is halfway through its cooking time, open the dome and carefully pour the prepared glaze over the ham.
11. Close the dome and continue cooking.
12. Once done, let the ham rest for about 10 to 15 minutes before slicing.
13. Serve hot.
14. Enjoy!

Lamb Recipes

53. Delicious Mustard Coated Leg of Lamb With Roasted Vegetables And Pistachios

Serving: Serves 2 - 3

Ingredients:

- 1 (1 1/2 pound) boneless leg of lamb, fat trimmed
- 1/2 turnip, large diced
- 4 baby Yukon gold potatoes, cut in half
- 1/2 celery root, large diced
- 2 large carrots, large diced
- 2 parsley roots, leaves removed and roots cut in half lengthwise
- 1 1/2 tablespoons extra virgin olive oil, divided
- 2 tablespoons pistachios, roasted and salted
- 1 tablespoon thyme, roughly minced
- 1 tablespoon Dijon mustard
- 1/2 ounce rosemary, roughly minced

- 4 garlic cloves, roughly chopped
- Freshly ground black pepper, to taste
- Kosher salt, to taste

Directions:

1. Place the Yukon potatoes, celery root, carrots, and parsley roots together in a large mixing bowl.
2. Add in the olive oil, black pepper, salt and thyme. Toss well until all the vegetables are coated in oil.
3. Add in the pistachios and transfer the mix to the liner pan.
4. Place the leg of the lamb on a dry and flat working surface.
5. Score the surface of the lamb using a sharp knife.
6. Spread the mustard on the fat side of the leg.
7. Sprinkle the rosemary, black pepper, garlic and salt over the leg of the lamb.
8. Place the seasoned lamb over the vegetables in the liner pan.
9. Cook on the HI setting for an hour or until the internal temperature of the lamb reads about 140 degrees and the vegetables are well browned and tender.
10. Serve hot.
11. Enjoy!

54. Roasted Lamb Chops With Feta And Olives

Serving: Serves 2

Ingredients:

- 1 tablespoon olive oil
- 1/2 tablespoon lemon juice
- 1 garlic clove
- 2 lamb chops, 1-inch thick
- 2 tablespoons chopped ripe tomatoes
- 2 ounces feta cheese, crumbled
- 2 - 3 pitted Kalamata olives
- Salt, to taste
- 1/2 tablespoon chopped parsley
- Freshly ground black pepper, to taste

Directions:

1. Combine together the olive oil, lemon juice and garlic together in a shallow mixing bowl.
2. Add the lamb chops to the bowl and toss well until well coated on all sides. Cover and refrigerate for 30 minutes.
3. In another small mixing bowl, combine together the feta, olives, tomatoes and parsley. Keep aside.
4. Place the marinated lamb chops on the 4-inch cooking rack and sprinkle the pepper and salt over the marinated lamb chops.
5. Roast on the HI power setting for about 14 to 15 minutes. Make sure to turn the chops over around the halfway mark.
6. When the lamb chops are done, divide the feta mixture into two equal parts and spoon it over the lamb chops.

7. Roast on the HI power setting until the cheese melts.
8. Serve hot.
9. Enjoy!

55. NuWave Style Shepherd's Pie

Serving: Serves 2 - 3

Ingredients:

- 1/2 tablespoon olive oil
- 1/2 large onion, grated
- 1/2 pound ground beef and lamb mix
- 1 large carrot, grated
- 1 tablespoon Worcestershire sauce
- 1 tablespoon tomato paste
- 2 - 3 ounces red wine
- 2 sprigs rosemary, finely chopped
- 2 sprigs fresh thyme, finely chopped
- 1/2 cup beef stock
- 1/2 egg
- 1 1/2 cups mashed potatoes, fresh or leftover
- 1 cup parmesan cheese, grated and divided
- Freshly ground black pepper, to taste
- Kosher salt, to taste

Directions:

1. Pour the olive oil into a 3-quart pot and heat on a high flame until the oil is lightly smoking.
2. Add the grated carrot to the pot and sauté for about 2 to 3 minutes or until the carrot is tender.
3. Add the onions to the pot and mix well. Sauté for about 3 to 4 minutes or until the onion becomes translucent.
4. Add the lamb and beef mix to the pot. Continue cooking for about 10 to 12 minutes or until the meats are well browned.
5. If there is too much fat, drain it.

6. Pour the tomato paste into the pot and cook for about 2 minutes or until the paste is caramelized.
7. Pour in the wine and Worcestershire sauce.
8. Continue heating on the high flame until slightly reduced.
9. Add in the beef stock and continue heating for about 12 to 15 minutes or until the broth thickens into a thick gravy.
10. Season according to taste with salt and pepper and take the pot off the heat.
11. Pour the mixture into a large 10-inch baking pan and cover.
12. Refrigerate for about half an hour.
13. In a mixing bowl, place the mashed potatoes, salt, 1 1/2 cup Parmesan cheese, egg and pepper together. Mix well until well combined.
14. Spoon the mashed potato mix over the meat mix and smooth using the back of a spoon.
15. Add the remaining cheese to the top of the pie and place the baking pan on the 1-inch cooking rack.
16. Bake at 400 degrees Fahrenheit for about 15 to 17 minutes or until the top potato is well browned.
17. Serve hot.
18. Enjoy!

56. Rosemary And Thyme Crusted Lamb Shanks

Serving: Serves 3

Ingredients:

- 3 lamb shanks
- 1 clove garlic, crushed
- 1/2 red onion, chopped
- 1/2 sprig fresh rosemary
- 1 tablespoon fresh thyme or 1/2 tablespoon dry
- 1 bay leaf
- 1/2 tablespoon Worcestershire sauce
- 3/4 cup vegetables stock (broth)
- 1/2 (14 ounce) can crushed tomatoes
- 1 1/2 tablespoon white wine
- 1/4 teaspoon pepper
- 1/4 teaspoon salt

Directions:

1. Arrange the lamb shanks in a single layer on the 4-inch cooking rack.
2. Cook on the HI power setting for about 8 minutes on each side or until the desired level of doneness is achieved.
3. Place the roasted lamb shanks in a large mixing bowl.
4. Combine the garlic, onion, rosemary, thyme, bay leaf, Worcestershire sauce, vegetable stock, crushed tomatoes, white wine, pepper and salt together in a small mixing bowl.
5. Pour the prepared marinade over the lamb shanks and toss well until the lamb shanks are well coated.
6. Place the lamb shanks, along with the marinade, in the liner pan.

7. Cook on the 7 power setting for about 3 to 4 hours.
8. Make sure to pause the oven at regular intervals to turn the shanks over to ensure even cooking.
9. Serve hot over a bed of mashed potatoes.
10. Enjoy!

57. Sweet And Sour Lamb Chops

Serving: Serves 2

Ingredients:

- 1/2 tablespoon red wine vinegar
- 1/4 teaspoon ground sage
- 1/2 teaspoon dark brown sugar
- 1/4 teaspoon garlic powder
- 2 (1-inch thick) lamb chops
- 1/4 teaspoon pepper

Directions:

1. Whisk together the red wine vinegar, ground sage, brown sugar, garlic powder and pepper together in a small mixing bowl.
2. Pour the prepared spice rub over the lamb chops and rub the seasoning into the meat using your fingers.
3. Place the lamb chops on the 4-inch cooking rack.
4. Cook on the HI power setting for about 6 to 8 minutes for medium cooked lamb chops
5. Serve hot with a side of mashed potatoes or roasted vegetables.
6. Enjoy!

58. Mustard And Thyme Crusted Lamb With A Tangy Mint Sauce

Serving: Serves 5 - 6

Ingredients:

- 1 medium boneless leg of lamb (about 2 pounds)
- 1 teaspoon freshly ground pepper
- 1 tablespoon kosher salt
- 2 tablespoons Dijon mustard
- 1 tablespoon chopped thyme
- 2 cloves garlic, finely chopped (about 1 tablespoon)
- 1 tablespoon chopped rosemary

For Sauce:

- 1 tablespoon granulated sugar; adjust as per taste
- 1/4 teaspoon ground pepper
- 1/2 tablespoon kosher salt
- 1/2 cup chopped fresh mint
- 1 tablespoon olive oil
- 2 tablespoons white wine vinegar

Directions:

1. Place the lamb on a clean, dry and flat working surface. Use a sharp knife to trim the extra fat from the lamb and make deep cuts in the thicker parts of the lamb.
2. Cover the lamb with a piece of plastic and use a meat tenderizer to flatten the lamb until it is uniformly thick.
3. Sprinkle generous amounts of salt and pepper on both sides of the lamb.
4. Combine the mustard, thyme, salt, garlic, rosemary and pepper together in a small mixing bowl.

5. Spread the spice rub over the lamb and place the lamb in an oven safe baking dish.
6. Cover the baking dish and refrigerate for a few hours.
7. Roll the lamb into a thick roll and fasten it in place using a kitchen twine. You can also directly place the lamb roll on the 1-inch cooking rack, with its seam side down, without tying it.
8. Roast on the HI power setting for about 18 to 20 minutes per pound of meat for medium doneness.
9. Flip the meat over around the halfway mark.
10. While the lamb roasts, prepare the mint sauce.
11. Pour about 2 tablespoons of water in a medium mixing bowl. Add in the salt, sugar and pepper and whisk well.
12. Add in the mint, oil and vinegar and continue whisking until smooth.
13. Taste and adjust the salt, pepper and sugar according to taste.
14. When the lamb is cooked, rest the lamb for about 10 to 12 minutes before slicing.
15. Serve hot with the prepared mint sauce on the side.
16. Enjoy!

59. Moroccan Style Lamb Burgers With An Orange And Olive Salsa

Serving: Serves 8

Ingredients:

- 2 2/3 pounds ground lamb
- 2 jalapenos, seeded and minced
- 2 cloves garlic, minced
- 4 tablespoons fresh cilantro, chopped
- 1 1/2 teaspoons ground black pepper
- 2 large shallots
- 2 teaspoons salt
- 1 teaspoon ground cumin
- 1 teaspoon paprika
- 8 burger buns, of your choice

Salsa Ingredients:

- 4 tablespoons extra virgin olive oil
- 2 tablespoons honey
- 2 tablespoons fresh lemon juice
- 2 cups chopped red onion
- 4 large oranges, peel and remove pith, cut oranges into ⅓ inch cubes
- 1/2 cup chopped pitted green olives

Directions:

1. Place the ground lamb in a large mixing bowl.
2. Add in the jalapenos, garlic, cilantro, ground black pepper, shallots, salt, cumin and paprika.
3. Mix well until all the ingredients are well combined.
4. Divide the lamb mixture into 8 equal parts and flatten to make 1-inch thick patties.

5. Grease the 3-inch cooking rack with some butter or spray it with some cooking spray.
6. Arrange the prepared burger patties in a single layer on the greased 3-inch cooking rack.
7. Cook on the HI power setting or at 400 degrees Fahrenheit for about 5 to 6 minutes per side for medium doneness. Increase the cooking time to about 8 to 10 minutes per side for well-done burgers.
8. In another mixing bowl, combine together the olive oil, honey, fresh lemon juice, red onion, orange cubes and green olives together.
9. Place the patties on the burger buns and spoon the prepared salsa over them.
10. Serve hot.
11. Enjoy!

60. Butter And Tarragon Stuffed Lamb Chops

Serving: Serves 3

Ingredients:

- 3 (2 inch) lamb chops
- 2 cloves garlic, minced
- 1/2 stick soft, un-salted butter
- 1/2 tablespoon fresh parsley, chopped
- 1/2 large shallot, chopped
- 1/2 tablespoon fresh tarragon, chopped
- 1/2 teaspoon salt
- 1/8 teaspoon ground black pepper

Directions:

1. Place the softened butter in a small mixing bowl.
2. Add in the garlic, parsley, shallot, tarragon, salt, and black pepper. Mix well until all the ingredients are well combined.
3. Spoon the mixture into the lamb pockets and hold them in place using toothpicks.
4. Arrange the lamb chops in a single layer on the 3-inch cooking rack.
5. Cook on the HI setting for about 6 to 7 minutes per side for medium rare done lamb chops.
6. Serve hot.
7. Enjoy!

Seafood Recipes

61. Crispy Oven Fried Catfish

Serving: Serves 2

Ingredients:

- 1 cup yellow cornmeal
- 1 teaspoon salt
- 2 tablespoons flour
- 1/4 teaspoon black pepper
- 1 egg
- 1/8 teaspoon cayenne pepper
- ½ pound catfish, cut into filets

Directions:

1. Place the cornmeal, salt, cayenne pepper, flour and pepper together in a mixing bowl. Mix well until all the ingredients are completely combined. Keep aside.
2. Crack open the egg in another bowl and whisk using a wire whisk until lightly frothy.

3. Dip the catfish filets in the egg and turn them over until the filets are well coated in egg.
4. Place the egg coated fish filets in the cornmeal mix and toss until completely coated.
5. Place the flour covered catfish filets on the 1-inch cooking rack and cook at 420 degrees Fahrenheit for about 25 minutes or until the crust turns golden brown.
6. Serve hot with a fresh salad and your favorite condiment on the side.
7. Enjoy!

62. Spicy Oven Grilled Salmon

Serving: Serves 2

Ingredients:

- 2 (6 ounce) salmon fillets
- Salt, to taste
- 1 teaspoon chili powder
- 1 tablespoon olive oil
- Freshly ground black pepper, to taste

Directions:

1. Combine the chili powder, pepper, salt and olive oil together in a small mixing bowl to prepare a spice rub.
2. Use your fingers to rub the prepared spice rub on the salmon filets.
3. Add the Extender Ring to the base if required.
4. Arrange the spice rub coated salmon filets on the 4-inch cooking rack in a single layer.
5. Grill on the HI power setting for about 8 to 10 minutes per side or until the fish breaks easily when forked.
6. Serve hot with the condiment of your choice.
7. Enjoy!

63. Pesto And Asparagus Topped Orange Roughy

Serving: Serves 2

Ingredients:

- 1/3 cup readymade pesto
- 1/8 teaspoon hot sauce
- 1 tablespoon fresh lemon juice
- 2 (6 ounce) orange roughy filets
- ½ pint cherry tomatoes, sliced
- 8 asparagus spears, trimmed to 4-inches
- 1 yellow crookneck squash, thinly sliced

Directions:

1. Place the pesto, hot sauce and lemon juice together in a small mixing bowl. Whisk using a wire whisk until the ingredients have emulsified.
2. Cut 2 12" x 12" pieces of heavy-duty aluminum foil and place them on a clean, dry and flat work surface.
3. Place 1 filet of the orange roughy in the center of the foil.
4. Sprinkle the pieces of fish with some salt and pepper.
5. Divide the pesto in four equal halves and spoon each quarter of the pesto over the seasoned fish filets.
6. Spread a layer of asparagus, squash and tomatoes on the layer of pesto.
7. Top with the remaining pesto.
8. Fold the foil over the fish and seal the packet of the fish.
9. Use a flat spatula to transfer the fish packets onto the 4-inch cooking rack.
10. Bake the fish on the HI power setting for about 12 to 14 minutes or until the fish can be easily forked.

11. Carefully open the foil packet and remove the fish from it.
12. Serve hot.
13. Enjoy!

64. Oven Grilled Tuna Steaks With A Peperonata

Serving: Serves 2

Ingredients:

- 4 (6 – 8 ounce) tuna steaks
- 2 green bell pepper, deseeded and large diced
- 2 large onion, cut into large chunks
- 2 yellow bell pepper, deseeded and large diced
- 4 garlic cloves, minced
- 2 red bell pepper, deseeded and large diced
- 6 tablespoons fresh rosemary, chopped
- 1 lemon, squeezed for juice (optional)
- 4 tablespoons parmesan cheese, grated (optional)
- Freshly ground black pepper, to taste
- Kosher salt, to taste

Directions:

1. Add the onions, salt, rosemary, lemon juice, green bell pepper, red bell pepper, yellow bell pepper, pepper, cheese and garlic to a large bowl. Mix well.
2. Wrap the 1-inch cooking wrap with some heavy-duty aluminum foil and spray some cooking spray over it.
3. Transfer the pepper and onion mixture onto the greased and foil covered rack.
4. Cook for about 13 to 15 minutes on the HI power setting.
5. Use a kitchen towel to pat dry the tuna steaks. Sprinkle pepper and salt on both sides of the tuna steaks.
6. Once the peppers and onions are done, place the seasoned tuna steaks over the cooked peppers and onions.

7. Cook for about 10 to 12 minutes on the HI power setting for medium done steaks, and bake for about 14 to 16 minutes for well-done steaks.
8. Transfer the tuna steaks onto serving plates and serve hot with a side of roasted peppers and onions.
9. Enjoy!

65. Noodle And Tuna Casserole

Serving: Serves 1

Ingredients:

- 5 tablespoons butter, divided
- 3 scallions, finely chopped and divided
- 1 1/4 cups flat egg noodles
- 1 1/2 tablespoons flour
- 1 3/4 cups milk
- 1/2 teaspoon Dijon mustard
- Salt, to taste
- 1/2 can tuna, drained and broken into small chunks
- Freshly ground black pepper, to taste
- 1/4 cup frozen peas
- Extra virgin olive oil, to taste
- 3/8 cup bread crumbs

Directions:

1. Fill a 2-quart pot with water and heat over a high flame until the water is boiling.
2. Once the water is bubbling, add the noodles to the boiling water and cook for about 6 to 8 minutes.
3. Use a stainless steel steamer basket to drain the noodles.
4. Spoon the cooked noodles on a sheet pan and spread into an even layer. Pour the extra virgin olive oil over the noodles and keep aside.
5. Place about 2 tablespoons of butter in a medium sized frying pan and heat over a medium high flame.
6. Once the butter has melted, add about ½ the scallions to it and cook for about 2 to 3 minutes or until the scallions have softened.

7. Add the mustard and flour to the pan and cook for about 2 minutes while constantly stirring.
8. Slowly add in the milk, while whisking constantly to ensure there are no lumps.
9. Continue heating until the milk starts bubbling.
10. Keep cooking the sauce for another 18 to 20 minutes or until the sauce thickens and coats the back of the spoon.
11. Taste and season the sauce using salt and pepper.
12. Pour the sauce into a large bowl.
13. Add in the tuna, noodles and peas. Mix well until all the ingredients are well coated by the sauce.
14. Pour the prepared mixture into a 7.5-inch by 4.5 inch by 3-inch loaf pan. Keep aside.
15. Place the remaining butter in a small frying pan and heat over a medium flame.
16. Once the butter has melted, add in the remaining scallions. Cook the scallions until soft.
17. Add the breadcrumbs to the pan and continue mixing.
18. Cook for about 1 to 2 minutes or until the breadcrumbs are well browned.
19. Pour the prepared breadcrumb mix over the tuna mix.
20. Place the prepared loaf pan on the liner pan and bake for about 18 to 20 minutes on the 7-power setting.
21. Serve hot.
22. Enjoy!

66. Zesty Salmon With Lemon And Fennel

Serving: Serves 1

Ingredients:

- 1 (6 ounce) salmon filets, skin on
- 1 lemon, remove the zest and juice on ½ and cut the remaining ½ in slices
- 1/2 fennel bulb
- 1 tablespoon extra-virgin olive oil, divided
- Freshly ground black pepper, to taste
- Kosher salt, to taste

Directions:

1. Tear two pieces of foil; each piece of foil should be bigger than the filet of the fish.
2. Rub a little oil on the foil and keep it aside.
3. Cut the fennel bulb into 4 equal pieces and remove its core. Slice it thinly.
4. Transfer the fennel slices to a medium bowl. Add in the lemon juice, salt, lemon zest, olive oil and pepper.
5. Toss until well coated and keep aside for about 10 minutes to marinate.
6. Divide the prepared fennel mixture into two equal parts and spoon onto the greased foil.
7. Use a kitchen towel to pat the fish filet dry and season using salt and pepper.
8. Place the seasoned salmon filet on the fennel mixture, with its skin side up.
9. Place about 2 lemon slices on each fish filet.
10. Fold the foil over the fish to create a loose packet and fold the ends to seal the packet.
11. Place the prepared fish packets on the 1-inch cooking rack and cook on the HI power setting for about 25

minutes or until the internal temperature of the fish reaches 145 degrees.

12. Serve hot.
13. Enjoy!

67. Instant Baked Shrimp

Serving: Serves 6

Ingredients:

- 12 large shrimp, frozen, peeled and deveined
- 1/8 teaspoon ground cumin
- 1 tablespoon dark chili powder
- 1/8 teaspoon ground ginger

Directions:

1. Combine the cumin, chili powder and ground ginger together in a small mixing bowl.
2. Transfer the spice mix to a salt shaker and keep aside.
3. Arrange the shrimp in a single layer on the 4-inch cooking rack.
4. Cook the shrimp for about 2 to 3 minutes on the HI power setting.
5. Carefully open the dome and sprinkle the seasoning on the shrimp.
6. Continue cooking the shrimp for another 6 to 7 minutes or until the shrimp become pink.
7. Serve hot with your favorite condiment on the size.
8. Enjoy!

68. Parmesan Topped Scallops

Serving: Serves 2

Ingredients:

- 8 sea scallops
- 2 teaspoons lime juice
- 2 tablespoons butter
- 1/2 cup grated parmesan cheese

Directions:

1. Extract the muscle on the side of the sea scallops. Wash the scallops well and pat them dry using a kitchen towel.
2. Divide the scallops in 2 separate oven safe ramekins or in 2 real scallop shells. (You can find these at party supply stores)
3. Place about 1 tablespoon of butter over the scallops in the ramekins or in the shells.
4. Divide the lime juice and pour it over the butter.
5. Spoon the Parmesan cheese over the lime juice in two equal portions.
6. Place the ramekins on the 4-inch cooking rack.
7. Bake for about 8 to 10 minutes on the HI power setting or until the cheese on top is well browned.
8. Serve the scallops in the ramekin immediately.
9. Enjoy!

69. Oven Grilled Shrimp In Chipotle Sauce

Serving: Serves 2

Ingredients:

- 1 pound shrimp, cleaned and deveined (about 11 to 12 pieces)
- 1 1/2 tablespoons chopped garlic
- 1/2 (15 ounce) chopped can tomatoes
- 1/2 small can chipotle sauce (whole chipotles blended into sauce)
- 1/2 cup cold water
- 1/2 small red onion, sliced

Directions:

1. Place the shrimp in the liner pan.
2. Top the shrimp with the garlic and tomatoes and mix well.
3. Add in the chipotle sauce and cold water. Mix well.
4. Top with the red onion.
5. Cook on the HI power setting for about 12 to 14 minutes.
6. Serve hot with the condiment of your choice.
7. Enjoy!

Vegetarian Recipes

70. Spinach And Ricotta Stuffed Jumbo Pasta Shells

Serving: Serves 2

Ingredients:

- 6 jumbo pasta shells
- 1/4 cup shredded parmesan cheese, divided (about 4 tablespoons)
- 1 cup ricotta cheese
- 5 ounces spinach, sautéed
- Salt, to taste
- 1/2 egg, slightly beaten
- Freshly ground black pepper, to taste
- 1/2 (26-ounce) jar spaghetti sauce, divided
- 1/2 teaspoon Italian seasoning

Directions:

1. Follow the instructions on the package of the jumbo shells and prepare the jumbo pasta shells. Drain from the water and keep them aside.
2. Place the ricotta cheese in a large mixing bowl. Add in about 2 tablespoons Parmesan, egg, pepper, spinach, salt and Italian seasoning.
3. Mix well until all the ingredients are well combined.
4. Spoon the prepared mixture into the cooked jumbo pasta shells.
5. Spread about 6 tablespoons of the spaghetti sauce in the bottom of a 4-inch by 4-inch baking pan.
6. Place the spinach and ricotta stuffed pasta shells in the baking pan.
7. Pour the remaining spaghetti sauce over the pasta shells and top with the remaining 2 tablespoons Parmesan cheese.
8. Place the baking pan on the 1-inch cooking rack and bake for about 15 to 17 minutes at 375 degrees Fahrenheit or until the cheese is bubbling and becomes brown around the edges.
9. Serve hot.
10. Enjoy!

71. Oven Roasted Chickpeas, Olives And Cauliflower

Serving: Serves 2 - 3

Ingredients:

- 3 cups cauliflower florets
- 4 cloves garlic, coarsely chopped
- 1/2 cup Spanish green olives, pitted
- 1/2 (15 ounce) can garbanzo beans (chickpeas), rinsed and drained
- 1/4 teaspoon crushed red pepper
- 1 1/2 tablespoons olive oil
- 1 1/2 tablespoons fresh flat leaf parsley
- 1/8 teaspoon salt

Directions:

1. Place the cauliflower florets, garlic, Spanish green olives and garbanzo beans together in a large mixing bowl.
2. Add the red pepper, flat leaf parsley and salt and mix well.
3. Pour the olive oil into the bowl and toss well to coat.
4. Empty the bowl into the liner pan and spread it into an even layer.
5. Grill the veggies for about 17 to 20 minutes at 400 degrees Fahrenheit or on the HI power setting or until the vegetables are tender and browned.
6. Serve hot.
7. Enjoy!

72. Oven Roasted Spicy Zucchini And Corn

Serving: Serves 2

Ingredients:

- 1/2 pound medium zucchini, cut lengthwise, further cut cross wise into 3-inch spears
- 1 (16-ounce) packages frozen corn
- 1 garlic clove, minced
- Salt, to taste
- 1 teaspoon chili powder
- 1 tablespoon olive oil
- Black pepper as per taste
- Lime wedges (optional)
- 1/4 cup chopped scallions (optional)

Directions:

1. Place the zucchini, garlic, olive oil, corn and chili powder together and mix well until well combined.
2. Season to taste with salt and pepper and toss again.
3. Transfer the vegetables to a silicone pizza liner or a cookie sheet.
4. Place the pizza liner or the cookie sheet on the 4-inch cooking rack and cook on the HI power setting for about 18 to 20 minutes or until the vegetables are tender and browned.
5. Serve hot topped with some scallions and lime wedges.

73. Garlic And Thyme Roasted Mushrooms

Serving: Serves 2

Ingredients:

- 1 (8 ounce) package button mushrooms or crimini, cut into quarters
- 2 cloves garlic, finely chopped
- 1 1/2 tablespoon olive oil
- 2 tablespoons fresh thyme, chopped
- Freshly ground black pepper, to taste
- Salt, to taste

Directions:

1. Place the olive oil, garlic, thyme, salt and black pepper together. Whisk well until well combined.
2. Place the mushrooms in a large mixing bowl and pour the prepared marinade over it.
3. Toss well until the mushrooms are well coated.
4. Place the mushroom in a single layer into the liner pan.
5. Grill the mushrooms for about 20 to 22 minutes at 350 degrees Fahrenheit.
6. Serve hot.
7. Enjoy!

74. Herbed Grilled Fingerling Potatoes

Serving: Serves 2

Ingredients:

- 1 teaspoon coarse salt
- 1/8 teaspoon finely chopped fresh thyme
- 1/8 teaspoon freshly ground pepper
- 1/8 teaspoon finely chopped fresh rosemary
- 1/2 tablespoon extra-virgin olive oil
- 3/4 pounds fingerling potatoes, scrubbed

Directions:

1. Combine the pepper, rosemary, salt and thyme together in a small mixing bowl. Keep aside.
2. Place the fingerling potatoes in a medium bowl and pour the olive oil over the potatoes. Toss well until well coated.
3. Sprinkle the seasoned salt over the oil coated potatoes. Toss the potatoes well until well coated.
4. Arrange the seasoned potatoes in a single and even layer on the 3-inch cooking rack.
5. Grill the potatoes at 350 degrees Fahrenheit for about 15 to 17 minutes or until the potatoes are grilled on the outside and softened on the inside.
6. Serve hot.
7. Enjoy!

75. Delicious Creamy Baked Sweet Potatoes

Serving: Serves 2

Ingredients:

- 1 tablespoon olive oil
- 1 tablespoon brown sugar
- 3 medium sweet potatoes (6 - 8 ounces each)
- 1 tablespoon unsalted butter, melted
- 1 tablespoon cream

Directions:

1. Pour the olive oil over the potatoes and rub it using your fingers.
2. Place the olive oil coated potatoes on the 3-inch cooking rack.
3. Bake the potatoes for about 35 to 40 minutes at 420 degrees Fahrenheit.
4. Once done, cool the potatoes until manageable.
5. Once manageable, slice the potatoes in half.
6. Scoop the flesh from two potatoes into a large mixing bowl, leaving about ½ inch of flesh attached to the skin.
7. Scoop out all the flesh from the last potato so that you have enough potato flesh in order to fill the remaining two potato skins.
8. Add the brown sugar, melted butter and brown sugar to the potato flesh. Mix well until the potato and sugar mixture is smooth.
9. Spoon the prepared mixture into the 4 potato halves and place the stuffed potatoes on the 3-inch cooking rack.
10. Bake for about 7 to 9 minutes at 400 degrees Fahrenheit.

11. Serve hot.
12. Enjoy!

76. Cheesy Cauliflower And Broccoli Gratin

Serving: Serves 3 - 4

Ingredients:

- 1/2 cup Italian-seasoned bread crumbs
- 8 ounces fresh broccoli florets
- 8 ounces fresh cauliflower florets
- 1 tablespoon olive oil
- 3/4 cup mayonnaise
- 1/2 cup shredded mozzarella cheese
- 1/2 cup shredded cheddar cheese
- 2 green onions, sliced
- 1/8 teaspoon cayenne
- 1 tablespoon Dijon mustard

Directions:

1. Place the breadcrumbs in a medium sized dish. Pour the olive oil over the breadcrumbs and mix well until the breadcrumbs are lightly moist.
2. Arrange the broccoli florets and the cauliflower florets in the steamer basket.
3. Place the steamer basket over a pot of boiling water.
4. Cover the basket and steam for about 5 to 8 minutes or until the florets are tender. Drain the water from the florets until dry.
5. Grease a 1-quart baking dish with some butter or cooking spray.
6. Place the steamed broccoli florets and cauliflower in the prepared baking dish.
7. In a separate mixing bowl, combine together the mayonnaise, onions, cayenne, cheese and mustard together. Mix well until all the ingredients are well incorporated.

8. Spoon the prepared mix over the steamed florets.
9. Sprinkle some breadcrumbs over the florets and place the baking dish on the 1-inch cooking rack.
10. Bake for about 25 to 30 minutes at 350 degrees Fahrenheit.
11. Serve hot.
12. Enjoy!

77. Oven Baked Tomato And Cheese Casserole

Serving: Serves 3 - 4

Ingredients:

- 2 tablespoons olive oil, divided
- 1/2 (14-ounce) can whole plum tomatoes, peeled and drained
- 1/2 cup bread crumbs
- 1/2 (14-ounce) can diced tomatoes, drained
- 1 clove garlic, minced
- 1 tablespoon olive oil
- 4 mini fresh mozzarella balls, cut into quarters (1/4 cup)
- 1/2 tablespoon melted butter
- 5 basil leaves, thinly sliced and divided
- Salt, to taste
- 1/2 tablespoon parmesan cheese, shredded
- Freshly ground black pepper, to taste

Directions:

1. Place the breadcrumbs and 1-tablespoon olive oil together in a medium sized baking dish. Toss well until the breadcrumbs are slightly moistened. Keep aside.
2. Pour the remaining olive oil into a large mixing bowl.
3. Add in the whole plum tomatoes, diced tomatoes, garlic, mozzarella balls, butter, basil leaves, Parmesan cheese, salt and pepper and mix well until well combined.
4. Grease an 8-inch by 8-inch dish with the remaining olive oil.

5. Pour the prepared tomato and cheese mix into the greased baking dish.
6. Top the mixture with the prepared breadcrumb and olive oil mixture.
7. Place the baking dish on the 1-inch cooking rack.
8. Bake for about 15 to 20 minutes at 350 degrees Fahrenheit or until the top gets crisp.
9. Serve hot.
10. Enjoy!

78. Grilled Herbed Winter Vegetables

Serving: Serves 4 - 5

Ingredients:

- 1/2 medium butternut squash, peeled and diced
- 1 pound baby potatoes, scrubbed and halved
- 1 medium red beet, scrubbed, peeled and diced
- 1 large onion, cut into 1-inch wedges
- Kosher salt, to taste
- 1/4 cup olive oil
- Freshly ground black pepper, to taste
- 1 large parsnip, peeled and cut into 1-inch pieces
- 1/2 pound Brussels sprouts, trimmed and halved
- 1/2 tablespoon finely chopped rosemary
- 1/2 tablespoon paprika
- 1/2 tablespoon finely chopped thyme
- 1 tablespoon parsley

Directions:

1. Place the butternut squash, baby potatoes, red beet, onion, parsnip and Brussels sprouts together in a large mixing bowl.
2. Add in the olive oil, kosher salt, black pepper, rosemary, paprika, thyme and parsley and toss well until well coated.
3. Transfer the olive oil and seasoning tossed vegetables to the liner pan.
4. Grill for about 30 to 40 minutes at about 400 degrees Fahrenheit.
5. Serve hot.
6. Enjoy!

79. NuWave Style Chive Topped Anna Potatoes

Serving: Serves 2

Ingredients:

- 1 medium russet potato, washed and cut into 1/8-inch slices
- Kosher salt, to taste
- 1 1/2 tablespoons butter, melted
- Chives (optional)
- Freshly ground black pepper, to taste

Directions:

1. Pour a little butter (about 1/2teaspoon) into the bottom of an 8-inch baking pan. Swirl the butter around to grease the bottom and sides of the baking pan.
2. Place the potato slices in the greased pan in a spiral pattern, starting from the outside and working towards the center.
3. Brush some butter onto the potatoes and sprinkle pepper and salt over the potatoes.
4. Repeat the steps 2 and 3 until all the potato slices have been arranged in the pan.
5. Place the prepared pan on the 1-inch cooking rack.
6. Cook on the HI power setting for about 35 to 40 minutes or until the potatoes are tender.
7. Remove the pan from the oven and sprinkle the chives over the potatoes.
8. Invert the potatoes on a serving plate and serve hot.
9. Enjoy!

80. Garlic Butter Hasselback Potatoes

Serving: Serves 6

Ingredients:

- 2 garlic cloves, smashed
- Butter, as needed
- 6 tablespoons olive oil, divided
- Saffron, as needed
- 6 Idaho potatoes

Directions:

1. Combine the garlic, butter and olive oil together in a small oven safe baking dish.
2. Place the baking dish on the 4-inch cooking rack and cook on the HI power setting for about 4 to 5 minutes.
3. Carefully extract the baking dish from the oven.
4. While the butter is melting in the oven, place the Idaho potatoes horizontally on a cutting board.
5. Starting on one end, slowly make thin slices, cutting about three quarters through the potatoes.
6. Place the potatoes on the 4-inch cooking rack and brush the prepared garlic butter over the potatoes.
7. Bake the potatoes on the HI power setting for about 60 to 70 minutes.
8. Serve hot with the condiment of your choice.
9. Enjoy!

81. Herb Roasted Russet Potatoes

Serving: Serves 2 - 3

Ingredients:

- 3/4 pound russet potatoes, scrubbed well and cut into quarters
- 1/2 tablespoon fresh thyme, minced
- 2 tablespoons extra virgin olive oil
- 1/2 tablespoon oregano, minced
- Kosher salt, to taste
- 1/2 teaspoon fresh rosemary leaves, minced
- Freshly ground black pepper, to taste

Directions:

1. Place the quartered potatoes in a large mixing bowl. Pour the olive oil over the potatoes and toss well until well coated.
2. Add the thyme, oregano, rosemary leaves, salt and pepper to the mixing bowl and toss well.
3. Place the herbed potatoes on the 4-inch cooking rack and bake on the HI power setting for about 10 to 12 minutes.
4. Flip the potatoes over and continue cooking for another 10 to 12 minutes.
5. Serve hot.
6. Enjoy!

82. Healthy Pinto Bean Burgers

Serving: Serves 2

Ingredients:

- 1/2 tablespoon sunflower oil, plus extra for brushing
- 1/2 garlic clove, finely chopped
- 1/2 onion, finely chopped
- 1/2 teaspoon coriander
- 2 ounces white mushrooms, finely chopped
- 1/2 teaspoon ground cumin
- 1/2 (15 ounce) can pinto or red kidney beans, drained and rinsed
- 2 slices provolone cheese
- 1 tablespoon fresh flat leaf parsley, chopped
- 2 ciabatta buns
- Salt, to taste
- All-purpose flour, for dusting
- Freshly ground black pepper, to taste

Directions:

1. Place the pinto beans in a medium sized mixing bowl. Use a fork or the back of a spoon to mash the beans until smooth.
2. Add the mushrooms, onions, garlic, oil, coriander, cumin, and parsley. Mix well until all the ingredients are well combined.
3. Divide the bean mix into two equal portions and sprinkle a little flour on each half.
4. Shape the bean mix into a patty that is about 1-inch thick.
5. Brush some oil on the patties and place them on the 4-inch cooking rack.

6. Grill the patties on the HI power setting for about 5 to 8 minutes on each side.
7. Place the cheese on the patties and continue cooking for another 2 minutes or until the cheese is melted.
8. Slice the Ciabatta buns into halves and place the patties in them.
9. Serve hot with toppings and sides of your choice.
10. Enjoy!

83. Cheesy Quesadillas

Serving: Serves 2

Ingredients:

- 4 (10 inch) flour tortillas
- 4 tablespoons chopped cilantro
- 3 cups white Mexican cheese
- 3 cups sliced sweet bell pepper (optional)
- Sour cream (optional)
- Salsa to dip (optional)

Directions:

1. Place two tortillas on the 4-inch cooking rack.
2. Sprinkle the cheese, sweet peppers and cilantro in equal amounts on both of the tortillas.
3. Top the tortillas with the remaining tortillas.
4. Secure the tortillas with toothpicks or place the 2-inch cooking rack over the quesadillas to ensure that the top tortilla doesn't fly off.
5. Cook on the HI power setting for about 4 to 5 minutes.
6. Flip the quesadilla over and continue cooking for another 3 to 4 minutes.
7. Transfer the quesadilla to the cutting board and slice it into 4 pieces.
8. Serve hot salsa or sour cream.
9. Enjoy!

Dessert Recipes

84. NuWave Style Orange Glazed Carrot Cake

Serving: Serves 3

Ingredients:

- 1 1/4 cups all-purpose flour
- 1/8 teaspoon ground nutmeg
- 1/2 teaspoon baking soda
- 1/8 teaspoon salt
- 1 teaspoon baking powder
- 3/4 teaspoon cinnamon
- 1/8 teaspoon ground cloves
- 1/4 cup vegetable oil
- 1 cup packed light brown sugar
- 1 egg at room temperature
- 1/2 teaspoon vanilla extract
- 1/6 cup unsweetened applesauce

- Zest from 1/2 orange
- 1/4 cup raisins (optional)
- 1 cup grated carrots
- 1/6 cup chopped pecans (optional)
- 1 – 1 1/2 tablespoons fresh orange juice
- 1/2 cup confections sugar, sifted

Directions:

1. Add the flour, baking soda, cinnamon, cloves, baking powder, salt and nutmeg to a large mixing bowl. Mix well until all the ingredients are well combined. Keep aside.
2. In another large mixing bowl, place the brown sugar, egg, vanilla, oil, applesauce and orange zest together. Whisk well until all the ingredients are well combined.
3. Pour the dry ingredients into the wet ingredient in parts, mixing well after each addition to ensure that all the dry ingredients are well incorporated.
4. Add the raisins, carrots and pecans to the batter and fold until just combined. Do not over mix.
5. Grease a 4-inch by 4-inch baking pan with some butter.
6. Pour the prepared cake batter into the greased baking pan.
7. Place the prepared baking pan on the 1-inch cooking rack.
8. Bake for about 40 to 45 minutes at 375 degrees Fahrenheit. Check if the cake is done by poking a toothpick in the center of the cake, if it comes out clean, the cake is done cooking.
9. While the cake bakes, pour the orange juice in a small mixing bowl.
10. Add the powdered sugar to the orange juice and whisk well until combined.

11. Once the cake is done, cool it in the pan for about 5 minutes before cooling it on a wire rack.
12. Pour the prepared orange glaze over the cooled cake and serve.
13. Enjoy!

85. Zingy Orange Crinkle Cookies

Serving: Yields 6 cookies

Ingredients:

- 1 cup all-purpose flour
- 1/4 teaspoon salt
- 1 teaspoon baking powder
- 3/4 cups granulated sugar, divided
- 1 egg
- 5 tablespoons butter, softened
- Zest from 1/2 orange
- 2 - 3 drops orange food coloring
- 1 tablespoon orange juice
- 1/4 cup powdered sugar
- 1/2 teaspoon orange extract

Directions:

1. Sieve together the flour, salt and baking powder together in a medium bowl. Mix well and keep aside.
2. In another bowl place the butter and add in about1/2 cup sugar to it. Cream the butter until the sugar is well incorporated.
3. Add the egg to the butter and sugar mix and whisk well until well combined.
4. Pour in the orange juice, orange food color, orange zest and orange extract. Mix well until well combined.
5. Slowly add the flour mix to the wet ingredients in 3 parts, mixing thoroughly after each addition to ensure that there are no lumps.
6. Use a scoop to scoop out about 6 even golf ball sized balls.
7. Empty the granulated sugar into a flat plate and roll the cookie dough balls in the sugar.

8. Sprinkle the powdered sugar over the sugar covered dough balls and place them in a silicon baking ring or a well-greased cookie sheet.
9. Place the baking ring or the cookie sheet on the 1-inch cooking rack.
10. Bake at 350 degrees Fahrenheit for about 12 to 14 minutes or until the edges of the cookies are golden brown.
11. Extract the cookies from the oven and cool them completely before serving.
12. Enjoy!

86. Chocolate Chip And Candy Stuffed Oatmeal Cookies

Servings: Yields 18 cookies

Ingredients:

- 1 1/4 cups old fashioned oats
- 1/4 cup granulated sugar
- 1 cup all-purpose flour
- 1/2 cup brown sugar
- 1/2 teaspoon baking soda
- 1/2 teaspoon salt
- 1/2 cup melted coconut oil
- 2 teaspoons vanilla extract
- 1 large egg
- 1/2 cup plain candy coated chocolate pieces
- 1/2 cup chocolate chips

Directions:

1. Combine the oats, granulated sugar, flour, brown sugar, baking soda and salt together in a large mixing bowl. Mix well until all the ingredients are well combined. Keep aside.
2. In a separate large bowl, pour in the oil, vanilla extract and egg. Whisk well until all the ingredients are well emulsified.
3. Slowly add the flour mix to the wet ingredients in 3 parts, mixing thoroughly after each addition to ensure that there are no lumps.
4. Add in the candy coated chocolate pieces and the chocolate chips to the batter. Fold until just combined.
5. On the 2-inch cooking rack, place a silicone baking ring.

6. Add the Extender Ring to the base of your oven.
7. Use a 1-inch cookie scoop to scoop out dough balls and place them at 1-inch intervals on the silicone baking ring.
8. Bake the cookies at 300 degrees Fahrenheit for about 14 to 16 minutes or until the cookies are light brown on the top.
9. Repeat the baking process until all the cookies are baked.
10. Cool the cookies completely before serving.
11. Enjoy!

87. Pink Champagne Cupcakes and Cake

Servings: Yields 6 cupcakes and1 (6 inch) layer cake

Ingredients:

Cake Ingredients:

- 1/2 box white cake mix
- 1/4 cup vegetable oil
- 1/2 cup pink Champagne
- 2 drops red food coloring
- 2 egg whites

Pink Champagne Frosting Ingredients:

- 1 (8 ounce) packages cream cheese
- 2 cups powdered sugar
- 1/2 stick butter
- 2 drops red food coloring
- 2 tablespoons Champagne

Directions:

Cake Directions:

1. Prepare the cake according to the instructions on the package, but just substitute the water with champagne.
2. Add a few drops of red food coloring to the batter and mix well until all the food color is incorporated.
3. Add about 1 cup of the batter to a greased 6-inch baking pan.
4. Place the 2-inch cooking rack upside down in the liner pan.
5. Place the prepared baking pan on the upside down cooking rack.
6. Place the 3-inch cooking rack over the cake.

7. Pour the remaining batter into cupcake liners to about the 2/3 full mark and arrange on the 3-inch cooking rack.
8. Add the Extender Ring to the base of the oven.
9. Bake at 350 degrees Fahrenheit for about 14 to 16 minutes or until a knife inserted in the center of the cake comes out clean.
10. Remove the cupcakes and the cake from the oven and cool on a wire rack before frosting.

Frosting Directions:

1. Place the cream cheese and butter together in a larger mixing bowl. Cream together until smooth.
2. Slowly pour in the champagne and add in the powdered sugar alternatingly until the mix is fluffy and light.
3. Add a little food coloring and mix well. Do not add too much as the frosting needs to be a very light and pale pink.
4. Once the cake and cupcakes are cool, frost them using a piping bag or a spoon.
5. Serve topped with some candy or sprinkles.
6. Enjoy!

88. Cinnamon And Honey Crackers

Servings: Yields 18 cookies

Ingredients:

- 1 1/2 tablespoons whole milk
- 1/2 tablespoon pure vanilla extract
- 1 tablespoon honey
- 1/2 cups all-purpose flour
- 1/8 cup granulated sugar
- 1/6 cup firmly packed dark brown sugar
- 1/4 teaspoon baking soda
- 1/8 teaspoon salt
- 1/8 teaspoon ground cinnamon
- 2 tablespoons unsalted butter, cut into 1/2-inch cubes and frozen

Directions:

1. Place the honey, milk and vanilla extract together in a small mixing bowl. Whisk well until all the ingredients are well emulsified and forma smooth mix. Keep aside.
2. Mix together the flour, baking soda, salt, sugar and cinnamon together into the jar of a food processor. Blitz until all the ingredients are well combined together.
3. Add the frozen butter pieces to the flour mix and continue blitzing until the mix has crumbly texture.
4. Slowly pour the milk mixture into the flour mix and continue blitzing it gets a doughy texture.
5. Remove the dough from the food processor and place on a flat, lightly floured work surface.
6. Cover the dough with plastic wrap and flatten the dough into a flat disk.

7. Refrigerate the dough for about 40 to 45 minutes.
8. Once the dough is chilled, remove the plastic wrap and transfer the dough on a flat work surface. Make sure you dust the surface with some floor.
9. Roll the dough until it is about 1/8-inch thick.
10. To the 3-inch cooking rack, add the silicone baking ring.
11. Use cookie cutters to cut the dough into desired shapes and transfer the cookies to the silicone baking ring.
12. Bake the cookies for about 8 to 10 minutes at 300 degrees Fahrenheit.
13. Cool the cookies in the tray for about 3 minutes before transferring them to a wire rack to cool.
14. Repeat with the leftover dough.
15. Serve warm if possible.
16. Enjoy!

89. Zingy Lemon Cookies Topped With Lemon Candies

Servings: Yields 24 cookies

Ingredients:

- 2 cups all-purpose flour
- 1/4 teaspoon salt
- 1/4 cup (1/2 stick) unsalted butter, softened
- 1 cup granulated sugar
- 1/2 teaspoon baking powder
- 1/4 cup shortening
- 1 teaspoon pure vanilla extract
- 1 large egg

Icing Ingredients:

- 1 cup powdered sugar
- 2 tablespoons milk
- 1/2 teaspoon vanilla
- 1/3 cup crushed lemon candies

Directions:

1. Sieve together the flour, salt and baking powder together in a large mixing bowl. Once well combined, keep aside.
2. In another bowl, add in the shortening, sugar, vanilla, butter and egg. Use an electric beater to cream together the ingredients on low speed.
3. Slowly add the flour mix to the butter and egg mix, stopping after each addition to ensure that the flour mix is properly incorporated and there are no lumps.
4. Continue mixing until you get a soft dough.
5. Divide the dough into 4 equal quarters.

6. Wrap each quarter in plastic wrap and refrigerate the dough for 4 to 6 hours or overnight.
7. Before baking, remove the dough from the refrigerator.
8. Leave the dough out until it reaches room temperature.
9. Place the dough between two sheets of plastic wrap and roll until it is about 1/8-inch thick.
10. Lightly dust a working surface with some flour and place the dough on it.
11. Cut the cookies from the sheet using your favorite cookie cutters.
12. Place the cookies on 1-inch intervals on the liner pan.
13. Bake at 300 degrees Fahrenheit for about 14 to 16 minutes or until the edges of the cookies start browning.
14. Rest the cookies in the liner pan for a few minutes before transferring the cookies to a cooling rack.
15. Repeat the steps from 7 to 14 to prepare the remaining cookies.
16. Make sure you cool the cookies completely before icing them.

Icing Directions:

1. Combine the powdered sugar, milk and vanilla together in a large mixing bowl.
2. Mix until the icing has the consistency of a spread.
3. Pour the prepared icing over the cooled cookies.
4. Serve topped with the lemon candies.
5. Enjoy!

90. NuWave Style Blueberry Muffins

Servings: Yields 12 muffins

Ingredients:

- 1 cup fresh blueberries
- 2 tablespoons margarine
- 1 cup all-purpose flour, divided
- 3/4 cup white sugar
- 1/2 teaspoon vanilla extract
- 1 egg
- 1/2 cup milk
- 1/2 teaspoon salt
- 2 teaspoons baking powder

Directions:

1. Sprinkle about 2 tablespoons of the flour over the blueberries and toss well until the blueberries are well coated in the flour.
2. In a separate mixing bowl, place the margarine. Slowly add in the sugar and whisk well until the margarine is creamed.
3. Add the eggs to the margarine mixture and whisk well until just combined.
4. Pour in the vanilla extract and mix well.
5. Add in the milk and whisk well. Keep aside.
6. Sieve together the flour, salt and baking powder in a small mixing bowl.
7. Pour the dry ingredients into the wet ingredients and fold until all the ingredients are well combined and there are no lumps in the batter.
8. Add the flour covered blueberries to the batter and fold.

9. Fill 12 silicone cupcake liners with the batter until they are about 2/3 full.
10. Place the muffins on the 1-inch cooking rack and bake at 350 degrees Fahrenheit for about 15 to 20 minutes or until a knife run through the center of the muffin comes clean.
11. Cool the cupcakes on a wire rack before serving.
12. Enjoy!

91. Raisin And Oatmeal Cookie Cake

Serving: Serves 6 - 7

Ingredients:

- 3/4 cup all-purpose flour
- 1/2 teaspoon ground cinnamon
- 1/2 teaspoon baking soda
- 1/4 teaspoon salt
- 1 tablespoon cornstarch
- 1/8 teaspoon nutmeg
- 1/2 cup margarine or butter, softened
- 1/4 cup granulated sugar
- 6 tablespoons firmly packed brown sugar
- 1/2 egg
- 1/2 cup golden raisins
- 1/2 teaspoon vanilla
- Frosting (optional)
- 1 1/2 cups old fashioned rolled oats

Directions:

1. Sieve together the flour, cinnamon, nutmeg, baking soda, salt and cornstarch together in a small mixing bowl. Mix well until well combined. Keep aside.
2. In the bowl of a stand mixer, place the margarine. Add in the granulated sugar and the brown sugar and whisk on the low speed until the butter is fluffy and light.
3. Add in the egg and vanilla and continue beating until all the ingredients are incorporated.
4. Slowly add in the previously sieved dry ingredients and beat well until you get a smooth and lump free dough.

5. Slowly add in the oats and raisins and mix well until incorporated.
6. Lightly grease a silicone pizza liner with some butter and press the dough into the bottom of the greased silicone pan.
7. Add the Extender Ring to the base of the oven.
8. Bake the cookie cake at 350 degrees Fahrenheit for about 22 to 25 minutes.
9. Extract the cookie cake from the oven and cool for a few minutes before flipping it onto a 3-inch cooking rack.
10. Carefully peel the liner pan of it.
11. Return the cookie cake to the oven and bake for about 15 to 17 minutes at 300 degrees Fahrenheit.
12. Once done, cool the cookie cake and cover with the frosting of your choice if you want.
13. Serve immediately.
14. Enjoy!

92. Dense Pound Cake With A Maple Syrup Glaze

Servings: Yields 1 loaf

Ingredients:

Cake Ingredients:

- 1/2 pound butter, softened
- 3 large eggs
- 1 1/2 cups sugar
- 2 cups flour
- 1 teaspoon vanilla extract
- 1/2 cup milk

Maple Glaze Ingredients:

- 2 tablespoons milk
- 1/2 cup powdered sugar
- 2 tablespoons maple syrup

Directions:

1. Place the butter in a large mixing bowl. Gradually add the sugar to it and cream well until the butter is smooth and creamy.
2. Add in the eggs and whisk until just combined. Add the eggs one at a time, whisking well after each addition to ensure that the egg is well incorporated.
3. Sieve the flour into the egg mixture and mix well until just combined.
4. Pour in the vanilla extract and the milk and mix well until it forms a smooth and uniformly thick batter.
5. Pour the prepared batter into a loaf pan or a 4-inch by 4-inch baking pan.

6. Place the loaf pan on the 1-inch cooking rack and bake at 3000 degrees Fahrenheit for about 50 to 60 minutes.
7. While the cake bakes, prepare the glaze.
8. Pour the milk in a small mixing bowl.
9. Add in the maple syrup and powdered sugar.
10. Whisk well until it gets a smooth glaze like consistency.
11. Once the cake is done, cool in the pan for a few minutes before inverting the cake onto a cooling rack.
12. Slice the cake and pour the prepared glaze over it.
13. Serve warm.
14. Enjoy!

93. Halloween Special Pumpkin Cheesecake

Serving: Serves 4

Ingredients:

- 1/2 cup granulated sugar
- 1/2 tablespoon all-purpose flour
- 1/2 teaspoon confectioners' sugar
- Pinch of ground cloves
- 1/4 teaspoon ground cinnamon
- Pinch of ground nutmeg
- 1 (8 ounce) package cream cheese, softened
- 1 egg at room temperature
- 1/4 cup canned pumpkin puree
- 1 (3 ounce) ready to use graham cracker crust
- 1/4 teaspoon vanilla

Directions:

1. Combine the granulated sugar, confectioner's sugar, flour, ground cloves, ground nutmeg and ground cinnamon together in a small mixing bowl. Keep aside.
2. Place the cream cheese in a large mixing bowl. Add in the pumpkin puree and whisk well until well combined.
3. Pour the prepared flour and sugar mixture into the cream cheese mixture and mix well until well combined.
4. Add the eggs to the flour and margarine mixture one at a time, whisking well after each addition to ensure that the eggs are well incorporated.
5. Pour in the vanilla and whisk until well combined.
6. Pour the filling onto the ready to use graham cracker crust.

7. Place the filled crust on the 2-inch cooking rack.
8. Add the Extender Ring to the base of the oven.
9. Bake the prepared cheesecake at 300 degrees Fahrenheit for about 40 to 45 minutes.
10. Place the cheesecake on the cooling rack.
11. When the bottom of the cheesecake is cool enough to touch, transfer the cheesecake to the refrigerator and cool for about 6 to 8 hours or overnight.
12. Slice the cheesecake into desired pieces and serve.
13. Enjoy!

94. Apple Crisp

Serving: Serves 4

Ingredients:

- 2 fresh apples
- 1/2 cup sugar
- 3/4 cup all-purpose flour
- 1/4 teaspoon salt
- 1/4 cup soft butter or margarine
- 1 tablespoon cinnamon
- Whipped cream

Directions:

1. Scrub and wash the apples well. Peel the apples and thinly slice them.
2. Place the peeled apple slices in the bottom of a 4-inch by 4-inch baking dish. Keep aside.
3. Sieve together the flour, salt, sugar and cinnamon together in a medium sized mixing bowl.
4. Add in the butter and lightly whisk until the mixture resembles coarse sand.
5. Sprinkle the prepared butter and flour mix over the sliced apples.
6. Place the baking pan on the 1-inch cooking rack.
7. Bake at 350 degrees Fahrenheit for about 30 to 45 minutes or until the top crust is brown.
8. Serve warm topped with a dollop of whipped cream.
9. Enjoy!

95. Fresh Pear Custard Pie

Serving: Serves 3

Ingredients:

- 1 1/2 pears, peeled, halved, sliced into 1/4-inch pieces
- 1/8 cup unsalted butter, melted
- 1/8 teaspoon nutmeg, plus extra for dusting
- 1/6 cup granulated sugar
- 1 teaspoon vanilla extract
- 1/6 cup all-purpose flour
- 1 1/2 large eggs
- 1/8 teaspoon salt
- 1/2 cup milk
- Confectioners' sugar (optional)
- Butter or non-stick cooking spray

Directions:

1. Grease the sides and the bottom of a 5-inch tart pan with the nonstick cooking spray or with butter.
2. Place the pear slices in a spiral in the greased tart pan, beginning from the outside and slowly working towards the center.
3. Sprinkle the nutmeg over the pears and keep the tart pan aside.
4. Place the butter, flour, eggs, salt, sugar, vanilla, salt and milk together in the jar of a blender.
5. Blitz for about 30 to 45 seconds or until the batter has a smooth consistency.
6. Pour the prepared custard over the pears.
7. Place the tart pan on the 2-inch cooking rack.
8. Add the Extender Ring to the base of the oven.
9. Bake on the HI power setting for about 35 to 40 minutes or until the custard is set.

10. Transfer the pie to a cooling rack and cool until just warm.
11. Flip the pie over to a serving plate and serve warm or chill before serving.
12. Enjoy!

96. Salted Chocolate Tart

Serving: Serves 5 - 6

Ingredients:

- 1 cup crushed sea salt potato chips
- 1/8 cup all-purpose flour
- 2 1/2 tablespoons unsalted butter, melted
- 5/8 cup heavy cream, divided
- 1/2 teaspoon vanilla extract
- 5 ounces semisweet chocolate morsels
- 1/8 teaspoon salt
- 4 ounces bittersweet chocolate morsels
- 1 large egg
- Sea salt for garnish

Directions:

1. Place the crushed sea salt potato chips, flour and melted butter together in the jar of a food processor. Blitz for about 30 to 45 seconds or until all the ingredients are well combined.
2. Transfer the prepared mix into a 5-inch springform pan and press it gently into the bottom and the sides of the pan.
3. Place the pan on the 4-inch cooking rack and bake on the HI power setting for about 5 to 7 minutes or until the crust is set. Keep it aside to cool.
4. Add about 2 tablespoons of the heavy cream to a small saucepan and heat over a medium low flame until the heavy cream is lightly bubbling.
5. Reduce the flame to low and add the semisweet chocolate morsels to the pan.
6. Stir constantly using a rubber spatula until the mixture is smooth and well combined.

7. Add in the salt and vanilla to the chocolate and cream mixture and mix well until well combined.
8. Add in the egg and stir well until the egg is well incorporated.
9. Pour the prepared chocolate mixture on the cool crust and smoothen the top using a spatula.
10. Place the Extender Ring on the base of the oven.
11. Place the pan on the 1-inch cooking rack.
12. Bake on the 8 power setting for about 15 to 17 minutes
13. Increase the power setting to the 9 power setting and bake for an additional 8 to 10 minutes or until the chocolate mixture is set.
14. Remove the pan from the oven and set aside to cool
15. Prepare the ganache by pouring the remaining heavy cream into a small saucepan.
16. Heat the heavy cream on a medium low flame until the cream is lightly bubbling.
17. Reduce the heat to a low and add in the bittersweet chocolate morsels.
18. Stir continuously until the chocolate and the cream is well combine and the mixture is smooth.
19. Pour the prepared ganache over the cooled pie and use a spatula to spread it into an even layer.
20. Refrigerate the pie 4 to 6 hours or overnight.
21. Slice into pieces and serve topped with a pinch of coarse sea salt.
22. Enjoy!

97. Tangy Orange And Buttermilk Cupcakes

Serving: Yields 6 cupcakes

Ingredients:

Cupcake Ingredients:

- 3/4 cups flour
- Pinch of salt
- 3/8 teaspoon baking soda
- 3 tablespoons unsalted butter
- 1/2 teaspoon vanilla extract
- 1/2 cup sugar
- 1/4 teaspoon orange extract
- 3/8 cup buttermilk
- 1 egg, room temperature

Orange Cream Frosting Ingredients:

- 1/2 (8 ounce) package cream cheese, room temperature
- 1 cup powdered sugar
- 2 tablespoons butter, room temperature
- 1 tablespoon orange extract
- Orange food coloring (optional)
- 1/2 tablespoon vanilla extract

Directions:

Cupcake Directions:

1. Sieve together the flour, salt and baking soda together in a small mixing bowl. Keep aside.
2. Place the butter in a medium pot and heat over a low flame until the butter has melted.
3. Add in the sugar and continue heating for about 1 minute, stirring constantly.

4. Take the pot off heat and add in the vanilla extract, orange extract and egg.
5. Mix well until well combined.
6. Gradually add the flour mix and the buttermilk alternatingly to the pan, starting and ending with the dry ingredients. Stir well after each addition to ensure there are no lumps.
7. Pour the prepared batter into 6 cupcake liners.
8. Place the prepared cupcakes on the 2-inch cooking rack.
9. Add the Extender Ring to the base of the oven.
10. Bake on the 8-power setting for about 13 to 16 minutes or until a knife run through the center of the cupcake comes out clean.
11. Open the dome of the oven and carefully remove the rack from the oven.
12. Cool the cupcakes for 5 to 7 minutes before removing the liners from the cupcakes.

Frosting Directions:

1. While the cupcakes cook, place the cream cheese and butter in the bowl of a stand mixer.
2. Beat slowly on the low speed until the butter and cream cheese are well mixed.
3. Slowly add in the confectioners' sugar, while constantly beating on the low speed, until all the sugar is well incorporated.
4. Add in the vanilla extract, orange food coloring and orange extract to the bowl. Continue whisking until well blended.
5. Spoon or pipe the prepared frosting over the cooled cupcakes.
6. Serve topped with some orange candy or sprinkles.
7. Enjoy!

98. Cherry Filled Cheesecake Cookies

Servings: Yields 18 cookies

Ingredients:

- 1 3/4 cups all-purpose flour
- A pinch of salt
- 1 (8 ounce) package cream cheese, softened
- 1 teaspoon baking powder
- 3/4 cups sugar
- 1 1/4 cups butter, softened
- 1 large egg
- 1/2 tablespoon orange liqueur
- 1/2 cup confectioners' sugar
- 1 teaspoon vanilla extract
- 1/2 cup graham cracker crumbs
- 1 (20 ounce) can cherry pie filling

Directions:

1. Sieve together the flour, salt and baking powder in a small mixing bowl. Keep aside.
2. In another bowl, place the cream cheese, sugar and butter together. Beat with an electric mixer for about 2 minutes or until the mix is creamy, fluffy and smooth.
3. Slowly add in the egg, orange liqueur and vanilla extract to the bowl. Continue whisking until well incorporated.
4. Gradually add in the confectioners' sugar and mix well until all the sugar is well incorporated.
5. Slowly add the prepared dry ingredient mix to the bowl and continue whisking until the ingredients are just combined. Do not over mix.

6. Cover the dough with a plastic wrap and refrigerate for about 45 minutes or until the dough is firm to touch.
7. Place a silicone baking ring on the 2 inch cooking rack.
8. In a wide and shallow dish add in the graham cracker crumbs.
9. Roll the chilled dough into 1-inch balls and then dredge the balls through the graham cracker crumbs until well coated.
10. Place the graham cracker crumb coated dough balls in the silicone baking ring, leaving about ½ inch space between 2 balls.
11. Lightly press the center of each dough ball.
12. Bake on the HI power setting for about 10 to 12 minutes.
13. Open the dome of the oven and carefully place about 3 cherries in the indentation on each cookie.
14. Close the dome and continue baking on the HI power setting for another 3 to 4 minutes or until the cherries are set.
15. Remove the rack from the oven and cool the cookies completely before serving.
16. Enjoy!

99. NuWave Style Raspberry Crumble

Serving: Serves 1

Ingredients:

- 2 tablespoons unsalted butter, softened
- 1/4 cup all-purpose flour
- 3/8 cup brown sugar
- 1/2 pint fresh raspberries
- 1 tablespoon cornstarch
- 1/4 cup sugar
- 1/2 lemon, juiced

Directions:

1. Place the butter, flour and brown sugar in a medium sized mixing bowl.
2. Mix the ingredients together using your hands, until the mixture resembles coarse sand. Keep aside.
3. In another mixing bowl, mix together the raspberries, cornstarch, sugar and lemon juice.
4. Pour the prepared raspberry filling into a greased ramekin and smooth out the top of the filling using a rubber coated spatula.
5. Sprinkle the prepared crumb topping over the raspberry filling.
6. Place the ramekin on the 2-inch cooking rack.
7. Add the Extender Ring to the base if required.
8. Bake on the 8 power setting for about 18 to 22 minutes or until the top crumb layer is golden brown.
9. Cool slightly and serve it warm.
10. Enjoy!

100. Paleo Style NuWave Chocolate Cake

Serving: Serves 3 - 4

Ingredients:

- 1/2 cup almond flour
- 1/2 cup cocoa powder
- 1/2 cup lentil flour
- 1/2 teaspoon baking soda
- 1/4 cup coconut oil, melted
- 1/4 teaspoon salt
- 2 eggs
- 3/8 cup honey
- ¾ teaspoon vanilla

Directions:

1. Pour a little coconut oil in a 4-inch by 4-inch baking pan. Swirl the pan around until the bottom and the sides are well coated.
2. Sieve together the almond flour, cocoa powder, salt, lentil flour and baking soda together in a large mixing bowl. Keep aside.
3. In another mixing bowl combine the eggs, vanilla, coconut oil and honey together and whisk well until all the ingredients are well incorporated.
4. Pour the almond flour mix into the bowl of a stand mixer.
5. Beat the ingredients with the whisk attachment on the low or medium speed.
6. While whisking, pour the wet ingredients into the bowl gradually. Stop every few minutes to scrape the sides of the bowl.
7. Continue whisking until the volume of the batter doubles.

8. Pour the prepared batter into the greased pan.
9. Place the pan on the 1-inch cooking rack.
10. Add the Extender Rung (3-inch) to the base of your oven.
11. Bake at 325 degrees Fahrenheit for about 35 to 40 minutes or until a knife run through the center of the cake comes out clean.
12. Remove the pan from the oven and cool the cake for about 10 minutes before turning it onto a wire rack.
13. Serve the cake warm.
14. Enjoy!

101. Berry Cream Pie

Serving: Serves 4

Ingredients:

- 1 unbaked 5 inch pastry shell (packaged or home cooked)
- 1/2 cup granulated sugar
- 1/2 cup flour
- Pinch of salt
- 1/4 teaspoon vanilla extract
- 1/2 cup sour cream
- 1/4 teaspoon almond extract
- 1/2 (6 ounce) container fresh raspberries
- 1/2 (1 pound) container fresh strawberries
- 1/2 (6 ounce) container fresh blackberries

Directions:

1. Place the readymade or homemade piecrust on the 4-inch cooking rack.
2. Bake the piecrust on the HI power setting for about 20 to 25 minutes.
3. Once cooked, remove the piecrust from the oven and set aside to cool to room temperature.
4. While the crust is baking, add the flour, salt, vanilla, sugar, sour cream and almond extract to a large bowl.
5. Whisk using a hand whisk or an electric beater until the batter is well combined and has a light creamy texture.
6. Add in the raspberries, strawberries and blackberries.
7. Gently fold making sure that the berries do not get muddled.

8. Pour the prepared mix onto the cooled piecrust and spread evenly. Smooth out the top of the pie using a spatula.
9. Add the Extender Ring to the base.
10. Place the pie on the 1-inch cooking rack.
11. Bake on the 8 power setting for about 40 to 50 minutes or until the pie is well set.
12. One done, place the pie on the cooling rack until cool enough to refrigerate.
13. Refrigerate until chilled before slicing.
14. Serve chilled.
15. Enjoy!

Conclusion

As you can see from this recipe book, the NuWave oven is quite a versatile kitchen appliance and can aid in prepping and preparing a wide variety of dishes; from breakfast to appetizers to mains and even desserts.

The best part about using the NuWave oven is that due to its revolutionary 3-heat technology, you do not need to add a lot of extra fats to your foods, while their nutrients are retained and the food cooks a lot faster.

So, not only is the NuWave oven versatile, it also cooks your food in a timelier and healthier fashion.

All the recipes in this book can be made quickly, do not require a lot of prep work, and use easily available local ingredients that you do not need to head to specialty stores to buy!

To conclude I would just like to say that the NuWave oven is not just an ordinary piece of equipment that will lay unused in your kitchen. Rather it is a handy device that has a great value in our world today, where we need our food to be easy to prepare, while being healthy too!

I would like to thank you once again for purchasing this book and I hope you find the recipes in this book helpful.

Cook healthy. Eat healthy. Stay healthy.

Made in the USA
Lexington, KY
23 May 2017